Advance Praise for *You've Got 8 Se...*

"After reading the first few pages, I could not put it down. An insightful and refreshing book that is a treasure trove of useful techniques on how to communicate more effectively and to the point, with amusing real life anecdotes that keep the reader engaged until the last page. A must-read for the corporate world—and the real world!"

—Jean Pierre Lacombe, Chief Global Markets,
Head of IFC Research, The World Bank

"I loved the book and will recommend it to colleagues. Whether you're a grizzled CEO or a new associate, you'll benefit from Paul's practical ideas and strategies. I've read a number of communication books over the years, but this one exceeded my expectations. Thoroughly enjoyable."

—Bill Adams, Chief Investment Officer,
Global Fixed Income, MFS Financial Management

"Great insight and advice to hone your communication skills for every situation. Invaluable for anyone with an important message to deliver."

—Steven Marshall, President,
U.S. Tower Division, American Tower

"This book provides fresh, actionable advice on how to make your point *quickly*, *succinctly*, and *memorably*, so your ideas get through the deluge of non-stop information. On the flip side, since you, too, are probably inundated with emails, meetings, and presentations that just seem endless: Do yourself a favor. Give everyone you know a copy of this very practical (and funny) book. I know I will."

—Erin Deemer, Vice President,
People Development, Biogen

"*You've Got 8 Seconds* teaches you to find the core of your message and make it memorable. Filled with powerful insights and humor, this is a must-read for anyone who wants to sell their ideas or themselves. I started using Paul's tools immediately, and urge you to do the same."

—Jon Peters, CEO, AthenaOnline

"Superb blend of practical tips, humor and storytelling. Paul provides real insights and memorable tactics on how to excel at communication in today's frenetic world. All presenters (and writers) should read this book."

—Marissa Poole, Head of Global
Scientific Communication, Sanofi Genzyme

"I loved this book! Humorous and insightful—it's a great read and the advice is spot on. A must-read for leaders or anyone who wishes to inspire, motivate, or persuade."

—Kelly Courtney, Advocacy Strategy Advisor,
United Nations

"Paul's book answers the question that should haunt all of us: 'In a noisy world, how do I ensure my message is heard?' For those fortunate enough to know Paul personally, his voice and years of experience echo throughout this book. The result is a practitioner's dream—a useful, step-by-step guide on how to beat the noise and ensure people take notice."

—Michael Glass, Vice President, Talent Management
and Development, Thermo Fisher Scientific

"Getting your message across in our information-saturated age is a real challenge. Paul Hellman's book is packed with great advice for leaders, and it's fun to read, too."

—Marshall Goldsmith, executive coach and
New York Times-bestselling author of Triggers

"If you want to become an exceptional communicator, this is your how-to guide. It should be mandatory reading!"

—Mark Jesty, Chairperson, IMS/Toronto

"*You've Got 8 Seconds* tackles everyday communication dilemmas in a straightforward, relatable and humorous manner. You'll find the strategies you need—and we all need this book more than we realize!"

—Alison Quirk, Executive Vice President,
State Street (retired)

"An easy, high-impact read that provides every executive with the tips and tools to effectively communicate up, down, across organizations, and with customers. With this book you'll maximize your impression on every audience.

—Dusty Tenney, President,
Brooks Life Sciences

"Do you want to be remembered and get results? Paul's witty approach and insightful tips give you the communication strategies to get heard in a world of constant distraction. If you want to succeed in your business encounters, this is a must-read."

—Maureen Clang, Vice President,
Leadership Development, Travelers

"There's no time to waste when it comes to improving the effectiveness of your communications skills. *You've Got 8 Seconds* is a vital addition to your tool belt that I heartily recommend."

—Bill McGowan, author, *Pitch Perfect*

"You need to manage your professional brand. Use the tactics in this book. They work."

—Charles Miller, Senior Vice President,
Leadership Development, Citi

"Paul provides a fast, easy-to-use approach to ensure that others get your message. His method helps you make your point quickly—and with greater impact."

— Sandy Rezendes, Chief Learning Officer,
Citizens Financial Group

YOU'VE GOT
00:00:08
SECONDS

YOU'VE GOT

00:00:08

SECONDS

COMMUNICATION SECRETS FOR
A DISTRACTED WORLD

PAUL HELLMAN

AMACOM

American Management Association
New York • Atlanta • Brussels • Chicago • Mexico City • San Francisco
Shanghai • Tokyo • Toronto • Washington, DC

Bulk discounts available. For details visit:
www.amacombooks.org/go/specialsales
Or contact special sales:
Phone: 800-250-5308
Email: specialsls@amanet.org
View all the AMACOM titles at: www.amacombooks.org

American Management Association: www.amanet.org

This publication is designed to provide accurate and authoritative information in regard to the subject matter covered. It is sold with the understanding that the publisher is not engaged in rendering legal, accounting, or other professional service. If legal advice or other expert assistance is required, the services of a competent professional person should be sought.

Library of Congress data available upon request.

ISBN: 978-0-8144-3830-5
EISBN: 978-0-8144-3831-2

HB 07.31.2019

For Karen,
who appears occasionally in this book as "my wife,"
but who has been, for so long, so much more.

For my father,
not in the book directly,
but whose wisdom lives on in its pages.

And for my children,
Rebecca and Noah,
who teach me new secrets all the time.

ACKNOWLEDGEMENTS

I'm grateful to my consulting clients—I've worked with some of you for a shocking number of years. Thanks for the opportunity to test and refine these techniques, and for not being at all surprised when they work.

Thanks to CNBC.com, especially Allen Wastler, and to boston.com for publishing my fast tips, and to all those who subscribe to these tips from my website, and then occasionally email me about their value.

Thanks to my agents Janet Rosen and Sheree Bykofsky. It's always a delight to work with you both.

I'm grateful to Ellen Kadin, probably the most responsive editor in NYC, and certainly the most collaborative. Also to Barry Richardson, Miranda Pennington, and Jenny Wesselmann for moving things along with such grace. And to Rosemary Kane Carlough, an old friend, whom I'm so pleased to be working with again.

Thanks to Aimee Levy, a gifted designer, always generous with advice.

A book is a long, complicated project. There are many at AMACOM I will never meet. You work behind the curtain in editorial, production, marketing, and creative. And you make books like this happen. Thank you.

ABOUT THE TITLE...

8 Seconds

In 2015, Microsoft did a study on attention spans.[1] The conclusion?

> *"You now have a shorter attention span than a goldfish . . . eight seconds."*[2]

Communication Secrets

Here's what is *not* a secret: First, you've got to capture attention. Then, you've got to keep it.

The trick is how to do that. The trick is what this book's about.

—Paul

CONTENTS

PART III
....
Capture Attention with PRESENCE   111

SHOULD YOU READ THIS BOOK?
WHAT IF YOU DON'T HAVE TIME?

"I tend to make up my mind about people within thirty seconds of meeting them."

—RICHARD BRANSON, founder of Virgin Group

Warning: Others Are Making Split-Second Decisions about You—Right Now

They're deciding whether or not to listen to you, or read your emails, or, in general, give you the time of day.

"Are you the speaker?" people sometimes ask me before a meeting.

"Yes," I say. "Or at least I'm going to pretend to be."

But the truth is, every person in that room is on stage, because you and I present ourselves every day. And even if you're working at home, the moment you get on the phone and say "hello," people will infer all sorts of things about you—your intelligence, your attitude—just by your voice.

Same thing with your emails.

The point is, small moments aren't so small.

Back to our meeting. Suppose it begins with self-introductions. A small moment? Maybe not.

When it's your turn, you say:

1. **"I'm Harriet."** But you speak softly, as if you were wanted by the FBI and you suspect that half the room is working undercover.

    Your volume speaks volumes. Speak up, send the message that your message is IMPORTANT.

2. **"I'm Harriet."** But while speaking, you fidget with your hair, or your jewelry, or you touch your face—these are known as grooming gestures. Not recommended, although preferable to fidgeting with other people's hair or faces.

3. **"I'm Harriet???"** You make routine assertions sound like questions by ending every sentence on a higher note. As if you believe that, in this universe, nothing is certain and you just discovered, much to your surprise, that you are, in fact, Harriett. Or at least you *could be* Harriet. The whole thing is bewildering . . .

The premise of this book is that people's attention spans are ridiculously short, that sometimes all you get is a moment, and that these moments count.

Let's seize them.

No Time?

Let's talk about your time. In the next 24 hours, everyone in your organization—in every organization—will do one of three things:

1. Talk
2. Listen
3. Pretend to listen

You definitely don't have time. No one does, it's the information age, which means you're flooded with meetings, emails, and breaking news, every second of every day.

But consider: your colleagues and clients don't have time either. For sheer survival, they'll screen out anything that sounds like noise.

Let's make sure that *you* get heard.

Back to the book: As you'll see on page xxi (How This Book Works), you don't *necessarily* have to read it in the traditional start-to-finish way.

You need something fast. *You've got 8 seconds.*

Pretending to Listen?

At a meeting, while others talk, your inner experience may look like this:

1. Why does everyone at this meeting, you wonder, have such enormous water bottles? How long is this meeting going to last?
2. Chocolate donuts! The ones on the table look tasty. But wait, you're on a diet. Oh, who cares?
3. Focus, focus, focus. Good.
4. Right now, you're extremely focused on the word *focus*.
5. Oh look, a tweet: "A wealth of information creates a poverty of attention, according to Herbert Simon."
6. Who's Herbert Simon?
7. You've heard rumors the company is about to be reorganized, or downsized, or sold, or something. How will that affect you?
8. Time for another donut.
9. Why are you even at this meeting? And who's that person over there? Is that Herbert Simon?
10. You just realized something bad, there are 79 slides left. Is it too late, you wonder, to go to clown college?

p.s. Herbert Simon was a Nobel Prize–winning economist, and one of the first to talk about the attention economy.

HOW THIS BOOK WORKS

3 Key Strategies, with 100 Tactics, Based on 25+ Years of Experience

I work with leaders at global companies. My focus? How to excel in high-stakes communications. For example:

Executives at a biotech company need to explain the company strategy to thousands of employees. If the employees don't get it, the strategy won't work.

Leaders at a consumer products company need to make a dynamic presentation to senior executives about the results of a complex project. The project took a year. The audience wonders, was it worth it?

Analysts at a mutual fund company need to tell a roomful of colleagues and executives why to buy a specific bond. Time to talk: one to two minutes.

The challenge is always the same: how to get heard, get remembered, and get results. I've developed three strategies. They work.

1. Focus
2. Variety
3. Presence

Focus doesn't just mean to say less, but also to design a compelling message. I'll show you several methods, including *fast-focus*™, which I use with leadership teams and individual executives to make their messages stick.

Variety means to be *slightly* different. With variety, you'll make routine info come alive, you'll know when to shift gears—from *announce* to *discuss*—and engage others with smart questions.

If you're giving a presentation, you'll stand out in the first few seconds.

Presence matters because there are certain people you listen to just because of their presence, and others you tune out. But what is presence? We'll look at 10 actions that you can use right away to boost your reputation.

The book illustrates these strategies with fast, fun, actionable tactics. Each tactic is self-contained, so it's easy to skip around. And there's a headline on top, so you know the point right away.

Let's get going.

Capture Attention with FOCUS

"If you have an important point to make, don't try to be subtle or clever . . . Hit the point once. Then come back and hit it again. Then hit it a third time—a tremendous whack!"

—WINSTON CHURCHILL

Roadmap for Part I, Chapters 1–4:

How do you design a message that gets heard, gets remembered, and gets results?

One solution: say less. For example, tell them what you're *not* going to tell them. Saying less requires practice, and we'll discuss some easy drills (chapter 1).

Fast-focus™ (chapter 2) is the methodology I use with leadership teams and individual executives to design critical messages. We'll go through it, step-by-step.

Then we'll look at designing messages for special situations, such as how to talk about your accomplishments without bragging, and how to give difficult feedback without getting pushback (chapter 3).

Words are the raw materials of a message, so we'll end this section with how to make your words sparkle, whether speaking or writing, even if you have writer's block (chapter 4).

| CHAPTER 1 |

Say Less

"In Maine we have a saying that there's no point in speaking unless you can improve on silence."

—EDMUND MUSKIE,
former U.S. Senator and Secretary of State

Don't Over-Salt

Detail is like salt. You can always add more. (If others want more, they'll ask questions.) But once in, you can't take it out.

Consider what your audience wants to know. But also, and every bit as important, what they don't want to know—because they've got no time, no interest, they're preoccupied with 10,000 other things, and they'd gladly pay you a boatload of money if you simply didn't tell them.

"Describe yourself," one CEO asks job applicants, "in three words or less."

What would you say? Probably not "wordy and repetitive."

But how focused are you?

"You seem to have 29 ideas at once," an exec told one of his managers. "And I feel like I'm hearing them all, right this minute."

Ever gotten feedback like that?

I work with several companies where executives, after taking a communication assessment, will gladly tell you their preferred styles. Each style has its own color.

Let's say you walk into an office and see the color red. That means, in essence, "Get to the point. Then get out."

But most execs aren't that direct.

Your boss probably hasn't asked you to say it in three words or less, or given you feedback about your 29 ideas, or flashed the color red in your face.

Maybe she hasn't said a thing about valuing conciseness.

Assume it.

Avoid Mentioning All Your Children—Ditto for Lists Longer than Three Items.

Imagine standing in front of a huge televised audience, with only a minute to introduce yourself. The stakes are enormous. You're running for U.S. President.

What do you say, and what do you leave out? That's a problem that you and I, on a smaller stage, face daily.

At a 2016 Democratic debate, one of the candidates, a former U.S. senator, told us that he had five daughters and one son. Fine.

Then he proceeded to name each one, plus tell us their occupations.

But after the first two daughters, he paused, as if he couldn't remember a single thing about daughter #3.

Now I've only got two children. But clearly, as you have more and more kids, at some point—I don't know the exact number—your mind turns completely to mush.

Then the candidate recovered: "Julia! Massage therapist!" (Luckily, daughters #4 and #5 were both in school, so they were quickly dispensed with.)

But here's the question, and it's the same one your audience has: why do we need all this info?

Sometimes, when providing information, you and I fall in love with the details, as if they were our children. We want everyone to know all about them.

But this candidate's main message was clear, without the details: "Look, if I can raise six kids, I can obviously run a country."

Meanwhile, at a 2016 Republican debate, one of the candidates, a current senator, said he'd eliminate five federal agencies. Then he proceeded to name each one.

Same trap. Same result.

He listed the Commerce Department twice, as if to say, "You can't just get rid of the Commerce Department once. Any idiot can do that. No, I'm going to get rid of it, and then I'm going to get rid of it again . . ."

If the details are too much for you, the speaker, to remember, your listeners don't stand a chance.

Tell Them What You're NOT Going to Tell Them

There's mystery in what people don't say. Let's use that to our advantage.

When you ask someone, "How are you?" you get the mysterious answer, "Fine."

No one says, "Well, my spouse just ran off with the plumber, and ever since she left, I've been despondent. Also, the upstairs sink hasn't been draining properly."

But in other conversations, the border between what to disclose vs. what not to, gets murky.

I recently patrolled that border with a group of research scientists, while working on their upcoming presentations. Every presentation lives, or dies, at that border.

We all know what it's like to be in the audience. I often advise clients to imagine an unpleasant dental procedure.

Suppose your presentation is 10 minutes. That's a 10-minute procedure. And if you're one of eight people presenting that day, you'd need to multiply those 10 minutes by eight dentists.

That's a long time.

The Gettysburg Address, as you've probably heard at least 272 times, was only 272 words—two minutes. You wouldn't need a dentist for that, just a hygienist, cleaning and flossing at breakneck speed.

Wouldn't you rather your audience think *That meeting was way too short, I wish there'd been another 37 PowerPoint slides!* than the opposite?

Then consider, there are different ways to "tell."

You already know the value of a preview (tell them what you're going to tell them) and a review (tell them what you've told them), although it's shocking how seldom we use these tools.

Here's something different: Tell them what you're NOT going to tell them.

A research scientist could say, "I'm not going to tell you about each of the 278 validation studies we ran. Let's just say it was complicated." Message: We didn't just pull this data out of a hat.

When it comes to either information or dentistry, less is more.

To Say Less, Measure

Recently, I got a sports watch as a gift. The watch measures all sorts of things when you're out running, or walking, or getting carried away to the nearest hospital.

Sometimes, before it displays any stats, the watch adds a comment. But not always.

Suppose on Sunday, I walk out to the driveway and pick up the newspaper. No comment. Not even, *"We can't believe you're up so early! Way to go!"*

And even when it adds a comment, like after a four or five-mile workout, the watch seems unimpressed. *"Nice effort,"* is all it says. I suspect it's being sarcastic.

But what I've noticed, since I've been measuring things, is that my workouts keep getting longer and longer. The act of measuring is not neutral; it changes behavior.

If you want to be more concise, let's measure that. Here's a possible workout:

- → *In one-to-one conversations*, talk less than the other person. Instead of rambling on and on, ask at least one thought-provoking question per conversation.
- → *In meetings*, speak in 30–60 second bites. Provide the headline news first, with details later, and only give details if asked. You'll be surprised by how much you can say in 30 seconds.
- → *When presenting*, slim down to 10 PowerPoint slides or less. And occasionally, lose the entire deck (PowerPoint tips, page 102).

You get the point. I'd like to say more but, according to my watch, I've got to run.

Say More

You may have the opposite problem. "I've gotten feedback," a manager told me, "to speak up more at meetings."

"What stops you?" I asked him.

"Others in the room—they've got more experience and expertise. So I think, *Why would they listen to me?*"

Ever feel like that? Who hasn't.

It's an editing problem, really. You're at a meeting, you have a thought, but before you can say "hello," you edit yourself: "Is that really worth sharing?"

Over the years, as an author, I've worked with editors at several publishing houses. Editors range from very encouraging to very critical.

One day, I heard about an editor who was beloved for his glowing comments. "Brilliant!" he'd tell an author. "I just love your whole book."

Meanwhile, my editor at the time had just sent back my manuscript. Almost every page was marked up in red: "You lost me here." "Is this section really necessary?" "This whole chapter needs a lot of work."

So editors run the gamut. Let's talk about your editor, the one inside your head who determines what you say and what you don't, the "border guard on the line between thought and speech."[1]

If your inner editor is too fierce, it's inhibiting. Try this:

Practice speaking nonstop for 60 seconds on a random topic. Do this alone, perhaps in your car going to work.

You don't need to stay on the topic, just begin there. Any topic will do, for example, your To Do list, a current career dilemma, or your beliefs about spaghetti sauce.

Just voice your thoughts, as they occur—forget about being coherent—even if your only thought is that you have no beliefs, really, about spaghetti sauce.

The goal: loosen your editor, spark your spontaneity. You'll never change your personality—why would you want to?—just your range.

More or Less? Give Appropriate Detail

What's appropriate detail? This is the key question to ask yourself, again and again.

Answer: depends on your audience.

Consider the first line of Ernest Hemingway's *The Old Man and the Sea*. Hemingway was famous for simple words and short sentences:

"He was an old man who fished alone . . . and he had gone eighty-four days now without taking a fish."

If you're a fisherman speaking to a fishing audience, they'll want more detail; non-fishers, less. Similarly, technical audiences often appreciate more detail; nontechnical audiences, less.

Here's what *The Old Man and the Sea* looks like, by the way, as a PowerPoint slide:

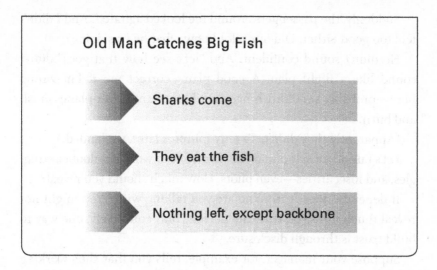

Hemingway chose to write a novel, not a Power Point slide.

Being concise doesn't mean speaking 24/7 in bullet points. Otherwise, you'll sound like a prisoner of war, or a terse teenager who thinks he's a prisoner of war.

So be flexible. And observe your audience. They'll give you clues about appropriate detail. When you're talking to someone and she starts tapping a pencil, or a foot, or the side of your head, that's a clue.

How Much to Self-Disclose? Stress-Test a Risky Disclosure

As we circled the Toronto airport, the pilot made a disturbing announcement.

He had to say something; we'd just attempted to land, then shot back up. So the passengers definitely needed an explanation, even if the pilot had to make one up.

"The problem," he said, in a somber voice, "is fog." That sounded like a perfectly good reason to me; I wish he'd left it there.

But then he added, "Several other planes are about to land. Let's see how that goes."

Suddenly, the passengers around me looked agitated. And I didn't feel too good either. Did our pilot know what he was doing?

He didn't sound confident. And "let's see how that goes" didn't sound like a flight plan. A good plan—correct me if I'm wrong here—probably shouldn't hinge on whether any other planes crash and burn.

(Apparently they didn't. Twenty minutes later, we landed.)

Let's talk about self-disclosure. Everyone at work has doubts, struggles, and insecurities—even pilots. How much should you reveal?

It depends, doesn't it? Who are you talking with? You might not reveal much until you trust the person. But, conversely, one way to build trust is through disclosure.

Suppose your manager, for example, tells you that she's working on being a better listener, and she'd like your feedback. Suddenly, she seems more human, more approachable. And you're likely to reciprocate.

Or a colleague confides over lunch about his struggles at home with work-life balance; you're likely to connect on a deeper level.

Here's another plus about self-disclosure: it's an effective way to make a point. Suppose our pilot, years later, teaches a course for new pilots: "How to Land an Airplane without Scaring All Your Passengers."

He might talk about that night in Toronto, and about his unease. "Even experienced pilots have doubts," he'd say. "I certainly did that night." That's good to hear if you're a new pilot.

But not if you're a passenger, in midair.

Stress-test a risky disclosure with two questions about your audience:

1. Upside: What does your audience gain by knowing?
2. Downside: How likely are they to want to jump off the plane?

CHAPTER 2

The Fast-Focus Method™

"I try to leave out the parts that readers tend to skip."
—ELMORE LEONARD, novelist and screenwriter

Be the Audience: Answer Their Three Questions

Most messages, spoken or written, are designed from the speaker's point of view. That's upside down. Imagine you're the audience. What would capture your attention?

Sometimes, I ask audiences what they're really thinking about. They say:

I'm thinking about my To Do list, and all the things I'm not doing, because I'm sitting here, half-listening to you.

Gluten. Why is everyone so obsessed with gluten-free food? Is gluten poisonous? I just ate a muffin. Did it have gluten? Am I going to die?

In one word: me.

The point is, your audience is probably not thinking about you. But to capture attention, you need to think about them. Be the audience.

Your audience, whether you're talking to 100 people at work or 1 person at home, has three questions, always the same.

Although these questions seldom get asked directly, they're the hurdles you have to jump, in sequence, to capture and hold attention:

1. Why should I listen (or read this)?
2. What exactly are you saying?
3. What should I do with this info?

To fast-focus your message, answer the three questions.

First Audience Question: Why Should I Listen?

Fast-focus with a purpose statement.

A purpose statement is like a present. You immediately hook people with something they value. It's a great way to start a meeting, phone call, or email.

Oprah Winfrey, years ago, gave each of her audience members a mysterious box. One of the boxes, she said, contained the keys to a new car.

Surprise—all the boxes did. Oprah gave away 276 new Pontiacs that day. Value: $7 million.

Want to capture your audience? You'll need a great present; what will it be?

"Not sure," you say, "because I don't have 276 Pontiacs. But wait, I do have 276 PowerPoint slides. Also some handouts."

Uh-oh.

If you watch Oprah that day, she looks as excited as the audience.[1] And if you walk in with a great present, you'll be excited too.

But how do you know if you've got something good? Well, like any present, it depends on the recipient—in this case, the audience. Oprah's audience had been specially selected; they really needed cars.

What does your audience need?

Once you've figured that out, tell your audience.

A strong purpose statement says what you're going to talk about and, more importantly, *why*. *Why* is the value, from the audience's perspective. *Why* answers the audience's question: "Why should we listen?"

Bad example: Suppose you're representing your company at a job fair. "My purpose," you say, "is to tell you why my company is the best place to work."

Well, that beats saying why it's the worst, although the latter might be more interesting. "Some of our products don't really work. A few smell bad. We think they may be carcinogenic."

It may be *your* purpose, as the speaker, to promote your company, but the audience has probably heard 20 other speakers say the same thing.

To figure out your purpose statement, take a few minutes to stop being you. Be the audience. What are their concerns?

Well, at the job fair, they're probably wondering what it's like to work at your company and if they'd like it.

Ok, start there. "Our purpose is to help you figure out if this company would be a good fit for you."

Maybe it would, maybe it wouldn't. But if you help the audience decide, you've given them a gift.

Your audience, it turns out, has absolutely no reason to listen to you. Give them one.

What If There's No Real Benefit? Tell Your Audience the Cost of Not Listening

Your proposition sounds like this: "Audience, if you listen, you'll either get something good, or else you'll *avoid* something bad."

Let's suppose you're talking about something uninteresting, for example, new regulations, to an audience that could care less. Your job: make them care more.

Maybe there's no real benefit to knowing about the regulations, but there's certainly a cost to not knowing. What is it?

Try opening your presentation with a picture: prison. "Our purpose today," you could say, "is to avoid going there."

Don't Confuse Your Purpose Statement with an Agenda

My client was unhappy. He'd just watched me present a two-day leadership workshop at his company, and he had only one comment.

"You should have asked the group a simple question, over and over," he said.

"What question?" I asked. I really had no idea. This happened long ago. Back then, I didn't think of myself as clueless, but not thinking you're clueless is probably one of the main signs that you might be.

Client: "What do these leadership skills have to do with selling more beer?"

His question sounded like, "So what's this got to do with the price of eggs?" I've never thought much about the price of eggs, even though I've heard the expression a million times. Apparently, some people are obsessed.

My client didn't care about eggs, and neither did the workshop group. They were sales managers, they sold beer, and what they thought about, all day long, was beer.

My mistake: forgetting the beer.

What's your audience thinking about? Let's assume they're preoccupied with 10,000 things. That's 10,000 reasons not to listen to you.

Unless you give them one. So give them one, with a purpose statement.

A purpose statement is not an agenda. Almost every executive I work with has an agenda—that's good—but a purpose statement is more important.

Agenda: "Today we'll talk about the seven practices of exceptional leaders, three big leadership mistakes, plus what the best leaders eat for breakfast and, if it's eggs, what's the price."

Your agenda is the *what*. It says, "Here's what I'm going to talk about." But it doesn't give the *why*. "Why should we listen?" your audience wonders. "We've got our own concerns."

Before you tell them the *what*, tell them the *why*. That's the purpose of a purpose. (True, I'm saying purpose a lot. On purpose.)

Your purpose needs to speak to their concerns.

Example: "Our purpose is to help you sell more beer. How? By inspiring your employees to sell more beer. By leadership."

Now give the agenda. And keep talking about the beer.

Second Audience Question: What Exactly Are You Saying?

Fast-focus with your main message.

"None of you will remember a single word I say today," the governor said. That's how he began his commencement address at my son's college graduation.

It was a memorable line. On the other hand, it raised a disturbing question: why listen?

Of course, technically, the governor was correct. If you're about to graduate college, and you've taken 30–40 courses, you already know an impressive amount about forgetting.

Let's edit the governor's opening. He could have said: "You won't remember anything I'm about to tell you. Except for ONE THING, and we'll get to that one thing in a minute."

If you say that, you create suspense. Then all you need is the ONE THING.

Unfortunately, a lot of other things work their way into a speech. The governor, for example, opened by thanking people. There was a list:

"Faculty, distinguished guests, undistinguished guests, the guests we really didn't want to invite but we sort of had to, the people we never even invited—hey, who's that funny looking guy over there? Sir, what are you doing here?"

Well, that's not exactly what he said. Too bad. Thanking people is a standard start, that's what makes it dull. Better: Jump right into your talk with an anecdote or a question, then later give the credits.

He ended with a call to action, along the lines of, "Serve and sacrifice." Nothing wrong with that, except it's easily forgotten.

Winston Churchill was alleged to have given one of the most memorable commencement speeches, and one of the shortest. Two years into WWII, 1941, Churchill reputedly said, "Never give in, never give in, never, never, never!"

That was the whole speech, then he sat down!

Or at least, that's the legend, which I'd heard—and spread!—before learning the whole story. Turns out, Churchill did say those words, but they were tucked into a longer, 740-word speech.[2]

Where did the legend of a one-line speech come from?

My guess is that "Never give in, never give in, never, never, never!" was the one line everyone remembered. And Churchill must have delivered it with "a tremendous whack" (as he advised others to do).

He knew the one thing.

Be Patient—Don't Expect Your Main Message to Pop Out of the Toaster, Ready-Made

You need to figure out what's *most important*, the main message, versus what's *secondary*, the key points.

Your discovery process might go like this: first, you brainstorm everything you want to say, on a whiteboard or Post-it notes, without even thinking about how it's organized. Then, you review your ideas, and sort them. What goes with what? What's most important? Do you see a main theme or a big idea?

Experiment with different arrangements. You might tag one of your ideas as the main message, then later decide, no, that idea is more secondary—it's a key point.

Eventually, a pattern will emerge. Once you've sorted and structured your information, you can visualize it like:

1. A solar system: picture the sun in the middle (your main message), then the planets (key points) around the sun, then a few moons (sub-points), near each planet.

To draw this, place your main message, center page, with a circle around it; then each key point in a smaller circle off to the side. (This is called a mind map.)

2. A tree: imagine the trunk is the main message; branches, the key points; twigs, the sub-points.

3. An organizational chart: display the hierarchy of your info with the main message on top, then key points and sub-points below.

The main thing is to know the main thing.

That way, when you walk into the boardroom expecting to deliver a 20-minute presentation, and the CEO says, "Sorry, you've only got 5," you know what to cut.

Because you know your main message.

Don't Confuse Your PowerPoint Slides with the Message

Sometimes I use slides, other times not, but one day, while designing a workshop called "*Managing Your Employees' Career Development*," I lost my way. Before identifying the main message, I plunged recklessly into the slides. I admit it, I fell in love with the slides.

Ever do that? You take all your info, slice and dice it into slides, and then play around with the sequence until, ok, it looks semi-coherent.

Your slide deck is done. But you're not, something's missing.

What's your main message? (True, you can figure it out after the slides, but you'll waste a lot of time that way.)

If you don't know the main message, your audience won't either, and by the time you get to slide #27 and say, "Hey, look at this pie chart," they'll be daydreaming. Probably about pastry.

Let's go back to my workshop, "*Managing Your Employees' Career Development*," and identify the main message.

How? *Be the audience.* Imagine, in this case, that you're a manager. What are your concerns about employee development? Possible concerns:

➡ You have *no promotions* or salary increases to offer, and that's what your employees really want.
➡ You have *no advice* to offer either. How can you tell someone what to do with his life when, most days, you can barely decide what clothing to wear?
➡ You have *no time.*

So, naturally, you'd rather avoid the whole thing.

But although your concerns are valid, your conclusion—*I've got nothing to offer*—is not. The main message should illuminate how to develop employees, despite constraints.

Main message: *Find coachable moments.*

This message needs to be developed, of course, into something that makes sense to your audience and is actionable. (More on coachable moments, page 76.)

You build the main message with key points. One key point could be about assignments—*every time you give an assignment, that's a coachable moment.* And you could expand this point with sub-points, what to do *before, during,* and *after* the assignment.

Your map now looks like this:

FIND COACHABLE MOMENTS

➡ Assignments
    Before assignment
    During assignment
    After assignment

You know your main message, and that gives you power. Because you can make it stick, with or without the slides.

Sequence Your Key Points so They're Memorable

Suppose you want people to remember the warning signs of a stroke.

There are five symptoms, according to the Berkeley Wellness Letter: difficulty speaking; numbness of face, arm, or leg; trouble seeing; trouble walking; severe headache.

Ok. Close your eyes and try to remember those symptoms. It's tough. But suppose you sequenced the symptoms differently?

This time, let's try a spatial sequence that moves down the body, head-to-toe:

1. Bad headache
2. Trouble seeing
3. Trouble speaking
4. Numbness of face, arm, or leg
5. Trouble walking

Suddenly, it's more memorable. Effective sequences often use time or space:

1. **Time: Chronological**—For example, what to do before, during, and after your next job interview.
2. **Time: Today, yesterday, tomorrow**—For example, our problem right now (today); how it began (yesterday); what we're going to do (tomorrow).
3. **Space: Large to small (or vice versa)**—For example, here's the forecast for the global economy, the U.S. economy, and our personal bank account.

Still remember those five symptoms of a stroke? Good. You can sequence your info in different ways, but it shouldn't be random.

When the Conversation Matters—Even if It's Fast—Know Your Main Message

"Work on your impact," an executive recently told me, "because, right now, you're not having any."

We'd just met, so he wasn't talking about me. He intended this feedback for an employee, but wanted to test it first.

"What do you mean by *impact*?" I asked.

"It means," he said, "*You need to collaborate more.*"

"And what does that mean?"

"*Speak up more at meetings,*" the exec said.

Good, now we've got a main message. Notice how, in a few drafts, we've gone from vague to specific. With feedback, your main message needs to be specific, otherwise it's likely to be misunderstood.

The exec could tell the employee, "You're smart and your ideas are good, so I'm always hoping you'll talk more at our meetings. What stops you?" Then, the two of them could discuss possible tactics.

How can you test your message? *Be the audience.* What will your audience hear, remember, and act on?

(For more on feedback, please see page 31.)

Keep Your Main Message Short and Simple— 10 Words or Less

"What's the single most important thing you want to say?" I asked a smart marketing exec.

"We're dedicated," she said, "to customer-centric, results-driven, streamlined solutions."

"Me too," I said. "Who wouldn't be? But what exactly does that mean?"

"Solve customer problems—fast," she said.

Much better. No one will recall the first version (do you?). It's short, but not simple. The second version, though, is easy to understand and easy to remember.

The key points could be about how you'll solve problems fast. For example, by doing the following:

➡ Hiring the best phone reps
➡ Being available 24/7
➡ Speaking really, really quickly

Your audience won't remember all the key points. They may not remember any. But you definitely want them to remember your main message. So keep it simple.

Reminder to Myself: Use Simple Words

One day, I was leading a workshop on executive communication when someone asked a simple question: "Should we do A or B?"

I was neutral. But instead of saying that, I said, "I'm agnostic."

Later, after the workshop was over, a participant walked over to ask what I'd meant by agnostic.

Apparently, he didn't know the word, or didn't get my usage. Or else he wanted to convert me to a religion where they speak simply.

Do you ever overcomplicate things?

Sometimes I'll read an article where the author—as if suddenly possessed—starts inserting German words like *doppelganger* or *schadenfreude*.

These words should all be verboten. Whoops, I meant forbidden. Let's stick to simple German words like *hamburger*.

The basic rule with foreign words: if you can't eat it, don't say it.

Speaking of food, here's a simple message about nutrition from author Michael Pollan: "Eat food. Not too much. Mostly plants."[3]

Actually that's three messages. The first, "eat food," means to avoid processed products. Still, the whole thing is seven words—and six are one syllable.

Try this: *Use words. Not a lot. Mostly simple.* (Michael Pollan's nutrition advice, version 2.0. Food for thought.)

Study Ad Slogans

While there's no reason for your main message to be a snappy ad slogan, we can still learn a lot from snappy ad slogans.

1. Talk like a regular person. "When it absolutely, positively has to be there overnight," promised FedEx.

The "absolutely, positively" part sounds like a real human being, worried about a real package.

FedEx could have used those 10 words from before ("Relax. We're dedicated to customer-centric, results-driven, streamlined solutions"). But that would have caused widespread panic.

2. Focus on one thing. Compare these two slogans from Wal-Mart:

a. "Always low prices. Always."
b. "Save money. Live better."

I like the first. A main message is one thing, not two or three. And I really like the repetitive "always."

For the same reason, "Sheer driving pleasure" (BMW) beats "Power, Beauty and Soul" (Aston Martin). Power, beauty, and soul add up to three abstractions—that's a laundry list, not a car.

3. Be concise. The best slogans from the past 100 years are under 10 words. Consider:

AVIS: *"We try harder."*
WENDY'S: *"Where's the beef?"*
APPLE: *"Think different."* And before Apple, the motto at IBM was simply *"Think."*

A short message is like Miller Lite beer: "Everything you always wanted . . . And less."

When Your Message Matters, Repeat It Multiple Times and Multiple Ways

One of my fears when traveling abroad is that I'll forget my passport, or lose it. Or else, in a desperate attempt to not lose it, I'll lock it in a hotel safe. And then forget it.

But on a business trip from Boston to Zurich, I had a different passport problem. When I went to check in, the ticket agent said I couldn't go.

"Your passport expires in a month," she said.

"But I'll be returning in a few days," I said.

"Doesn't matter. Your passport is completely unacceptable," she said. Her tone implied that neither she nor Switzerland was terribly disappointed.

Although I've traveled abroad dozens of times, apparently it's always been within the first 9.5 years of my 10-year passports. (Some countries, it turns out, require a six-month leeway.)

Your passport may be real, but the expiration date isn't. If milk worked this way, you'd never buy it. "This milk expires in 10 days," you'd say. "It's completely unacceptable."

Later that night, after driving home, I polled some friends and colleagues: "Did you know about this passport business?" Some did, others didn't. ("Are you sure you didn't do something to offend Switzerland?")

It made me wonder: how do you and I learn things like this? Or, to flip the question, suppose you needed to communicate an important message, like this one, to a large audience. How would you do it?

Well, you could:

➡ Make an announcement: The government, for example, could just send everyone a nice letter, or mention it on the passport application, or stamp it right on the passport itself: "Expiration date? SOONER than you think."

➡ Dialogue: A company could direct their corporate travel agent to ask each person about her passport before booking any trips.

The agent would ask, "So, when do you think your passport expires?" And then say, "Hmm. Switzerland has a different opinion."

➡ Tell a story: An ordinary person could tell a cautionary tale like mine, and then rely on word of mouth or social media to spread the word.

Each method has limits. Too often, we assume that it's enough to make an announcement—that if we just say it, others will hear it and remember it.

Someone must have announced something about this passport business. But I didn't hear it. Or else I heard it, but didn't remember it.

What's the shelf life of an announcement? Less than milk.

Third Audience Question: What Should I Do with This Info?

Fast-focus with a call to action.

Sometimes you go to a meeting and it's just an update. Nobody wants you to do anything with the info, they just want you to know about it.

Update meetings are useful, occasionally. But if most of your meetings are like that, you've got to wonder: is this really the best use of my time?

A call to action spells out the next step. It's usually about *doing* something. But if that doesn't fit, the next step could be to *think* something or *feel* something.

Suppose you're a CEO, giving an update after a tough week. Your call to action could be:

➡ What to think: "If you only remember one thing, remember this: our legal department is the best in the business."

➡ What to feel: "Feel proud about all of our products that are not, currently, in class action lawsuits."

➡ What to do: "Buy more stock—the price can't drop any lower."

Make Your Call to Action a Verb

Suppose you're giving a talk about the importance of setting ground rules before starting a project, or a meeting, or a challenging conversation.

Compare these two endings:

1. Ground rules are good.
2. Use ground rules.

Number 1 is an observation. Ground rules are good, but so are lots of other things. Goals are good, a To Do list is good, and drinking milk is good too. Number 1 is basically a greeting card.

Number 2 is a directive. It's got power.

The Fast-Focus Method™: Summary

Key principle: Be the audience.

Most messages and presentations are designed from the speaker's point of view. That's upside down. Imagine you're sitting in the audience. What would capture your attention?

Every audience has three questions	To answer the questions, use these tools:
1. Why should we listen? (What's in it for us?)	1. Purpose statement
2. What exactly are you saying?	2. Main message
3. What should we do with this info?	3. Call to action

Focus your opening, body, and close:

a. The opening

Purpose statement: Answers audience question #1:
Why should we listen?

The purpose is the hook that entices the audience to pay attention.

Example: "Our purpose is to increase your competence and confidence every time you speak." (All the examples on this page are from my workshop on *Dynamic Speaking*.)

Agenda: The agenda says how you'll accomplish the purpose.

Example: "We'll practice how to design and deliver a dynamic message."

b. The body

Main message: Answers audience question #2:
What exactly are you saying?

If your audience could only remember one thing, what's the one thing?

Example: "The single most important thing is . . . ENERGY."
Keep your main message short—10 words or less.

• KEY POINTS

The key points develop your main message.

Example: "When you design a message, ENERGY means to focus on your audience, and on why they should listen. When you deliver it, ENERGY means to vary your body language, vary your voice. When you feel uneasy, ENERGY means to accept your anxiety and use it."

c. The close

Call to action: Answers audience question #3:
What should we do with this info?

Close your presentation on a powerful note. What's the next step? What should the audience do?

Example: "Go out and practice, practice, practice. Then, practice some more."

Note: If there's nothing to *do*, then the call to action can also be: what to *think* (e.g., "If you only remember one thing, remember . . . ") or what to *feel* (e.g., confident . . . or excited . . . or proud, etc.).

The President of the United States called me the other day. I wasn't in, so he left a message. Let's critique it.

He's a skilled communicator. We'll analyze the pluses and minuses:

1. Intro: He opened with, "Hi, this is the President. I rarely make these calls, and I apologize for intruding on your day."

Plus: If you're the President, you probably should mention that. Adds credibility.

Minus: Apologizing. A lot of people open presentations with a disclaimer. "I rarely do this," they say. "I'm a little unprepared" or "I don't really work here."

My advice: don't.

2. Purpose statement: "I had to talk to you about the election in Massachusetts because the stakes are so high."

Plus: "You" is a wonderful word to use when presenting. It keeps the presenter focused on the audience.

Minus: Unfortunately, he emphasized the word "election." If he had emphasized "you" ("I had to talk to you"), it would have sounded more personal.

I began to wonder, does he even know who I am? Or is he just calling everyone in the entire state?

3. Main message: The President endorsed a specific candidate for Senate.

Plus: It's important to have a main message, 10 words or less. There were three key points supporting the main message, which is just right. Three is a good number: three strikes and you're out, three meals a day, The Three Stooges.

I could go on, but that's three examples.

4. Call to action: "A lot of people don't realize there is an election on Tuesday. They don't realize why it's so important . . . So please, come out to vote . . ."

Plus: Clear, specific action.

Minus: The phrase, "a lot of people don't realize" could be a nice way of saying that a lot of people are complete idiots. On the other hand, I did know there was an election, so I felt ok about that.

One last thing: The President forgot to leave his number. He's probably wondering why I haven't called back.

Three More Ways to Focus

"Everything should be made as simple as possible, but not simpler."

—ALBERT EINSTEIN

Only Got a Minute? Start with Your Conclusion

Imagine that your job is to analyze bonds. You work for a global money management company, and every day, you go to a fast-paced morning meeting with 30+ colleagues and senior executives.

You've got one to two minutes, at most, to speak about a particular bond.

Here's what your audience wants to know: *Should we buy the bond, or not—and why?* What they don't want: irrelevant details.

Sounds simple, but takes skill and practice.

One of my consulting projects was to work with these analysts. I asked the chief investment officer, Bill Adams, who runs the morning meetings, "What does a good message sound like?"

"Simple," Bill said. "First, give me your conclusion. Then tell me how you got there. Then give me your conclusion again."

The next time you're speaking (or writing) to senior executives, begin at the end.

Talking about Your Accomplishments?
Tell a Story

Sooner or later, someone's going to ask you what you've accomplished. You could be anywhere—a job interview, a performance appraisal, a parole hearing.

What's an accomplishment, anyway? Consider the following:

a. Getting out of bed (on a day when you were really sleepy)
b. Making $1 million
c. Performing brain surgery

An accomplishment needs three things: obstacles, skillful action, results. In other words, you take action, overcome obstacles, and get results. By that measure, none of the list items definitely makes the cut.

a. Getting out of bed has obstacles, and plenty of them, but that's about it.
b. Making $1 million could qualify. But maybe you took a $10 million business and ran it into the ground. Or maybe you won the lottery.
c. Brain surgery sounds impressive. When people try to reassure you about other tasks, they say, "Look, it's not brain surgery." That calms you down, unless you happen to be a brain surgeon:

> DOCTOR: So, what's on the schedule today?
> ASSISTANT: In 10 minutes, you're doing brain surgery.
> DOCTOR: Oh, no!!!

Is brain surgery an accomplishment? Well, what were the results? Did you actually get the brain back in the head? How's it working?

To make your accomplishments work, tell their story. But stay focused—use the acronym SOAR.

S is the Situation; here's where you describe the context. OAR refers to that trio we discussed previously: Obstacles, Action, and Results. These three pull your accomplishment along.

Suppose, for example, you worked as an account exec at a PR firm, and you happened to be my daughter, who, at the time, was just out of college. An accomplishment might sound like this:

- ➡ Situation: Needed to get PR for an important client; no one had been successful despite lots of effort.
- ➡ Obstacle: Client was thinly covered by the media, and the few reporters covering it kept getting reassigned.
- ➡ Action: Identified new media targets, developed relationships, and persisted.
- ➡ Result: Scored two important media meetings for the client's CEO. Client was so pleased that they increased the PR budget.

SOAR will focus your story. If you stick to what happened, you're not bragging, just reporting.

And remember, it's not brain surgery.

Giving Feedback? Try the XYZ Format

"My neck," the manager said, "is on the guillotine."

This manager had an influence problem. It involved a project team that didn't report to him, but he was accountable for the results.

I was coaching him on what to say. His first draft: "When a project goes bad, I feel distraught, because of my neck . . ."

Years ago, I learned, and then modified, a method for stating your case from an excellent book: *People Skills*[1]. The format (modified) sounds like this: "When X happens, I feel Y, because of Z."

X is the problem; Y, your reaction; Z, the business impact.

Let's critique the guillotined manager's XYZ:

X: "When a project goes bad."

Plus: His X avoids attacking or blaming. He didn't say,
"WHEN YOU SCREW UP A PROJECT."
Minus: What does he mean by "a project goes bad?"

I picture food that's gone bad. No longer recognizable, it's buried in the office refrigerator like an archaeological relic.

You wonder, what food group could this possibly have belonged to? It's best not to wonder, either about food or messages.

Let's be specific. What the manager really meant was, "When we miss a deadline."

Fine, say that.

Y: "I feel distraught."

Plus: Saying how you feel tells others that the issue is important.

Minus: "Distraught" is too emotional for business. It's like saying, "When we miss a deadline, I FEEL SO ABANDONED BY YOU."

That's heavy.

What's a business-appropriate emotion? Try *concerned.*

You can be concerned that the project is late, concerned that customers will be unhappy, concerned that, in a moment of despair, you'll probably eat the mystery food in the fridge and die of food poisoning.

Concerned covers it all with grace and, well, without any cause for concern.

Z: "Because my neck is on the line."

Plus: Authentic.

Minus: The business impact should be larger than any of your body parts, or whether or not you, individually, look good.

Better: "Because our reputation is on the line" or "because, if we miss a deadline, that hurts our customers."

Let's pull this XYZ together: "When we miss a deadline, I get concerned about the effect on our customers."

That's focused.

| CHAPTER 4 |

Watch Your Words—and Your Emails

Q: (What's) the one thing a gate agent should never say?
A: "Unfortunately." At JetBlue, we say "As it turns out."

—Interview with ROBIN HAYES,
CEO of JetBlue (*Wall Street Journal*, 8/10/16)

"I don't believe in email. I'm an old-fashioned girl. I prefer calling and hanging up."

—CARRIE BRADSHAW (from HBO's *Sex and the City*)

Avoid Jargon

"Do you want to hear about the 16 perils?" the salesperson asked me.

"Not especially," I said. I'd initiated this phone call, with a well-known company, to get a competitive bid on home insurance. My policy was up for renewal.

But the salesperson's approach surprised me. "Is your current policy," he asked, "an HO-3 or an HO-5?"

I had no idea. HO-3 sounded like HO-HO-HO. It was industry jargon, meaningful to the agent, but gobbledygook to everyone else.

"Why don't I just tell you what an HO-3 covers," he said. (The 16 perils!) "Then you and I can brainstorm whether anything is missing."

Brainstorming seemed like a shaky way to buy insurance, sort of like going on a quiz show: "Guess what's missing from this policy? That's right, FLOOD INSURANCE!"

33

But maybe it was a good way to sell insurance because, let's face it, the minute you think about your house being vandalized, or burned to the ground, or whirled away by tornados, you definitely want vast quantities of insurance.

So eventually, he read the 16 perils. I noted there was nothing about snakes. That was disappointing; I'm very motivated to avoid snakes and would definitely buy a HO-HO-HO policy that offered a no-snakes guarantee.

I decided to get another quote.

The next (and last) salesperson never mentioned HO-3 and never mentioned the 16 perils. But she did ask at least 16 questions about my house.

Her message: We're going to thoroughly understand your home so we can give you the right protection. (*Be the audience.*)

And I took it. Even though there was nothing about snakes.

Avoid Most Acronyms

The other day, I came across the acronym HOMES, which is supposed to help you remember the five Great Lakes.

I'd completely forgotten about HOMES. The truth is, I don't think about the Great Lakes as often as I should. They're obviously important, why else did we memorize them?

But even after I saw HOMES, I still couldn't name them all. I decided to do some research.

"Can you name the Great Lakes?" I asked my wife.

She proceeded to rattle off all five.

"How'd you do that?" I asked.

"Simple," she said. "HOMES."

Clearly, some acronyms work for some people.

My problem with HOMES is that it's got nothing to do with lakes, unless your home is completely flooded—"Let's get out of here, honey, all the rooms are like lakes!"—or you happen to live in a houseboat.

An acronym for the Great Lakes should be relevant, like WATER, or DROWN. Either one would work just fine, we'd simply have to rename most of the lakes to fit.

That's the thing about acronyms: they're often a forced fit.

But a few make sense. SMART spells out five criteria for an effective goal (Specific, Measurable, Achievable, Relevant, and Time-bounded). No force fit there; *smart* goals sound right and are used everywhere.

I like SOAR, which I just used a few pages back.

MADD, Mothers Against Drunk Driving, works despite the misspelling. MADD is emotional, which makes it memorable, and the emotion fits the crime.

I also have a soft spot for Fannie Mae and Freddie Mac, which are creative acronyms—nicknames really—that sound less like mortgage agencies and more like a pleasant couple you'd meet at a square dance. Perhaps near the Great Lakes.

But in general, the world is cluttered with acronyms—over 5 million, according to acronymfinder.com. Pick up any business book, and you're bound to run into some bad ones.

Use acronyms sparingly. Not everyone loves them, and some people, when they hear one, just don't feel at HOMES.

Use Strong Words

"Your years of service are appreciated," a manager told me recently.

Unfortunately, he wasn't referring to my years of service, since we'd only just met a few minutes earlier.

I had asked him, and the other managers in the workshop I was leading, to write a motivational message to an employee.

The problem with this manager's message: passive voice. We don't know who's doing the appreciating. And the only thing being appreciated is time. Apparently, his employee clocked in year after year, after year.

A stronger message to this employee: "I really value your expertise and know-how. For example, last week when you . . ." (provide an example or two).

How strong are your messages?

Passive voice, in writing, takes the life right out of a sentence. But passive voice is not just a writing problem.

Do you ever speak with a passive voice?

Let's consider four examples involving Henry, a hypothetical bank robber:

1. "I'll try to rob the bank," Henry says.

From a writing standpoint, that's ok. But when spoken, it's weak.

Try is a tip-off that Henry will never rob the bank. He'll probably never even go into the bank, he won't even use the ATM. Soon, Henry will be asking you to lend him money, saying he'll try to pay you back soon.

Good luck with that.

2. "The bank was robbed," Henry says.

By whom? This is classic passive voice. Henry has vanished from the sentence. Sure, he robbed the bank, but now he refuses to take credit.

3. "My stupid boss made me rob the bank," Henry says.

Don't you just want to go up to Henry, shake him, and say, "Henry, for god's sake, stop blaming other people in the organization. Take responsibility for your life, man."

4. "I robbed the bank."

Finally, Henry has spoken with an active voice.

And in 10–20 years, when Henry is released from jail, perhaps his boss will be there to thank him for his years of service.

Are you a leader? Of course you are. So then sound like one. Not "mistakes were made," but "I made mistakes, and here's what I'm doing to fix them."

Otherwise, you rob energy.

Swearing at Work?

A U.S. CEO was rebuked by his board for "salty language".[1] I read the story over breakfast, while abroad.

The breakfast was a buffet, lots of choices, and the woman at the next table was conflicted. She began with noble intentions: a dry omelet and a few rice cakes. Rice cakes, if you've never tried them, are similar to eating Styrofoam packaging material, but with less calories.

She nibbled at the omelet, nibbled at the rice cakes, then pushed her plate as far away as possible and got up.

A few minutes later, she returned with a new plate featuring an impressive stack of pancakes and several juicy strips of bacon.

If Freud had been there, he would have noted the never-ending struggle between what he called the id (your raw drives) and the superego (your disciplined, controlled side).

The problem with swearing at work is that it looks like you've got a loose, out-of-control id. But work is about control, starting each day when the alarm goes off—oh, no!—and you force yourself out of bed.

Does that mean that you should never swear, that you should commit instead to a restricted, rice cake–like verbal diet?

At some companies, swearing is the norm. A woman exec told me her male colleagues used to chide her for *not* swearing. She finally left.

Let's assume that's not the norm where you work. Consider your choices:

- Swearing at others. This one is easy: don't.
- Swearing to impress others. People with a high need for power, noted psychologist David McClelland, often use provocative language.
  The motive here is simply to get a reaction. It doesn't really matter to you whether others like you or your language.
  But maybe it should.
- Swearing at a situation. There are "moments in life," says psychologist Steven Pinker, "when the point for politeness has passed."
  Imagine a bad day. First, your computer crashes. Then the stock market crashes. Then your airplane crashes. At some point, you might say something stronger than darn.

But here's the thing. If you're a leader, people notice everything you do, from what goes into your mouth to what comes out.

And everything you do communicates your standards.

Lose Your Train of Thought? Try These Words

Suppose you're in the middle of a presentation when, suddenly, you can't think of a certain word, or you lose your train of thought. Maybe you've misplaced the entire railroad.

Perfectly natural, happens to everyone.

So you reach for a filler word, such as *um*. Nothing wrong with an occasional *um*. No one will notice unless, for some reason, they're counting every *um* you utter, which, I admit, is an intriguing hobby.

But it doesn't need to be yours.

Getting to zero *ums* should not be your life's work. Actually, if you never say *um*, you'll sound scripted and robotic. The goal: keep your *ums* under the radar. A few *ums* will go undetected.

There are worse filler words. For example: *like* or *you know*. Worse because they get noticed faster. Consider *like*.

Good use: "This tastes like potato salad."

Personally, I'd like to know if this really is potato salad, because maybe it started out as something entirely different, such as apple strudel, and then took a bad turn.

But from a usage perspective, we're fine.

Bad use: "I told my girlfriend that I like really loved her, and she was like, 'I like you too,' and I was like, 'I don't want to be liked. In fact, I really dislike that.'" (*Like* appears five times; only two are correct.)

Now let's look at *you know*.

Good use: Let's say you're at a party, and your host says, "You know Dorothy, don't you? Dorothy makes that wonderful potato salad."

And you say, "Of course I know Dorothy!" while thinking, *Dorothy? Who's Dorothy?*

Bad use: "It's, you know, embarrassing when you can't remember someone, you know?"

Both *you knows* are unnecessary. If we say, "It's embarrassing when you can't remember someone you know" (without the comma), that's better. We're obviously talking about Dorothy.

There are better words than *um*. Try these filler words instead: *well, now, so, and*.

For example: "Um, you must be Dorothy" becomes "Well, you must be Dorothy."

You can overuse any word. Sometimes I overuse *so*. So do others. *So*, reports the *New York Times*, is the new sentence opener.[2]

But just because everyone says so doesn't make it ok. In other words, "So what?"

Eventually, you may want to go beyond filler words. The simplest solution when unsure what to say next: pause. Pausing marks you as a calm professional.

Even if it feels strange, like you just ate some dubious potato salad.

Write ~~Bad~~ Badly

"I've got writer's block," an executive tells me. She's got to deliver a five-minute speech to 500 people, and she hasn't written a thing.

But she knows what she wants to avoid.

"I don't want to be clichéd, predictable, or boring," she says. "Or too dramatic, or too rehearsed. Also, I don't want to wear the wrong shoes."

That's the problem, and it's got nothing to do with footwear. Her internal editor is out of control.

Internal editor? Remember the one we discussed earlier (page 7, *Say More*)? It's your natural concern that everything you write, or say, be excellent. Having an internal editor is essential, except for one thing: it screws up the early stages of creating anything.

Writing is difficult enough, even for accomplished authors. "The struggle with writing is over," wrote Philip Roth, author of 31 books, on a Post-it note to himself. He'd finally decided, at almost 80 years old, to retire. "I look at that note every morning, and it gives me such strength."[3]

Anyone who writes anything—a report, a proposal, a fortune cookie—knows the struggle.

I struggle with birthday cards, even though the entire point of buying a birthday card is to get someone else to express your sentiments.

But you've still got to write something.

The solution to the writing struggle is always the same: get something down on paper—anything. Anything beats nothing.

How to start?

➡ Write without stopping (similar to the earlier advice about speaking nonstop). Set a time limit, say five minutes, and then keep your hands moving on the keyboard, or your pen moving across the paper, even if it's only to write:

    a. "I have nothing to say. Absolutely nothing. Furthermore, I still have nothing to say."
    b. "Paul's advice is completely useless."
    c. "Happy birthday, you're 49 years old! A year from now, you could be dead! Have a nice day."

➡ Talk it out. Instead of writing, speak into your smart phone's dictation app, or leave yourself a long voice mail. Sometimes it's easier to talk than write. But talk without stopping.

➡ Commit to writing badly. Make that your goal. The worse your writing is—spelling mistakes, bad grammar, incoherent thoughts—the better.

When you let yourself write badly, you loosen up and the words flow. Then, but not before, you've got something to edit.

All writing is rewriting. That's the best writing advice I ever got. But first, you've got to get something down. Create first, edit later.

Sharpen Your Emails by 10

1. Capture attention with your subject line.

"Are you about to date a convicted felon?" asks a recent email.

That's an intriguing question, spiced with romance and danger. I'm tempted to pluck this email right out of my spam folder and read it.

But I don't.

Why should anyone read your emails? There are 1,000 reasons not to, starting with the 1,000 other emails in everyone's inbox.

Every email competes for attention. Asking a question is one way to capture it.

2. Update your subject line.

"Let's postpone today's call." That subject line—for a call later today that's not being postponed—was originally written for last week's postponed call. And then never changed.

Updating the subject line is like changing your underwear. Do it at least daily.

3. Manage your emotions.

"I just read your stupid, stupid tip," emailed a reader, apparently unimpressed by my work. "I can't believe you feel good about writing something as stupid as that, and publishing it no less."

Please don't send emails when you're upset—let's assume your message will be forwarded to everyone and last forever—even if what you're upset about is how many stupid, stupid emails you're getting.

4. Don't email everyone.

205 billion emails were sent and received in 2015—daily.[4] You probably feel like you received most of them.

Reply to all? Please don't.

5. Avoid most abbreviations.

J = joking; IJ = I'm joking; YMBJ = you must be joking.

YMMV, which means "your mileage may vary," and also, more loosely, "your results may vary," is the "most popular slang looked up today."[5]

For example: "Whenever I date a convicted felon, it's always very exciting. YMMV."

Do you assume everyone knows these abbreviations? YMBJ.

6. Follow up.

You send someone an email but don't hear back. Don't assume the other person got it, opened it, read it, understood it, or remembered it.

And don't assume their lack of response means anything personal, or anything at all, other than they're drowning in a tsunami of 205 billion emails a day.

So follow up a few days later. And when you do, try something different (see #7).

7. Consider the phone.

Yes, email is fast, but sometimes a phone call, or short hallway conversation, is faster.

Sometimes putting a note in a bottle and hurling it out to sea feels faster than playing email ping pong all day.

And don't forget the old-fashioned letter. No one sends them anymore, which means no one's getting 205 billion of them. Your message will be read.

8. Respond.

Respond to emails quickly. Even if it's just to let the other person know you won't be responding quickly.

9. Adapt your style.

When you email, you're operating from one of two styles: letter-writing or texting.

a. If you're a letter-writer, like me, you dress up your emails with greetings and closings. And you write in sensible paragraphs. I usually start with *Hi*, which is the email version of *Dear*. I miss *Dear*.

b. If you're a text person, you're not going anywhere near *Hi* or *Dear*, but you might do an occasional *Hey*.

Suppose you email me: "Hi Paul, I just read your stupid, stupid tip. Cheers!" That sounds warmer than "Hey stupid."

But the point is to adapt your style to the other person. If you send me an email with *Dear*, I'll probably write *Dear* back. And if you skip the greeting, I'll do the same.

10. Edit, edit, edit.

Get right to the point in the first sentence or two. If you've got additional info, consider adding a paragraph called "details."

For example: *I'll be out of the office for the next few years.*

Details: *Last night, I dated a convicted felon—he'd just escaped!—and after an exciting, all-night car chase, we ended up in a Mexican prison. I'll be back in the office, assuming good behavior, in 5–10 years.*

Ok, you're out of the office. That's the main thing.

| PART II |

Capture Attention with
VARIETY

"I want to look back and know that I was terrible at a
variety of things."

—JON STEWART,
writer, producer, director, actor

Roadmap for Part II, Chapters 5–10:

Change wakes people up. Let's use that to our advantage.

Be slightly different (chapter 5) means to vary your style, without risking your reputation. You might, for example, vary your speed—in writing and speaking—or use three different ways to persuade.

Ever try to explain your job to someone outside your field? Try an analogy—it's one of the best ways to explain anything (chapter 6).

Stories are another way to stand out. But your story needs to deliver a business-relevant point. Here's my easy 2.5 Step Method™ (chapter 7).

Sometimes the most attention-grabbing tactic, when speaking, is to stop speaking and get others engaged. But knowing what's open for discussion, and what's not, trips up many leaders (chapter 8).

One way to engage others is with smart questions. Whenever you ask a question, that's an eight-second moment; others assess you by your questions. We'll talk about how to ask the best questions and how to answer the worst (chapter 9).

Variety matters in all communications, but it's critical in presentations. Let's energize your next presentation with a few tricks, including how to open, how to own the room, and why you should definitely talk about food (chapter 10).

CHAPTER 5

Be Slightly Different

"His socks compelled one's attention without losing one's respect."

—H. H. MUNRO,
writer

Be the Lightbulb Guy

One day, I was presenting a workshop when, suddenly, a stranger walked in, unfolded a ladder, and climbed to the ceiling. He wasn't trying to amuse us, he needed to fix a light.

Still, we couldn't take our eyes off him. He was like a circus act.

What made him so compelling? Variety—he broke the routine of the workshop. Sure, we'd seen people fix lights before, but not that day. Plus, he had a ladder. Never underestimate the power of a good prop.

But then, after a few minutes, he was still doing the same thing and we lost interest.

In retrospect, he should have ditched the ladder and performed his feat atop a team of acrobats or a herd of wild elephants. We'd have watched for a few more seconds.

Variety! Why does it work? Well, a zillion years ago, if you were in the jungle and you heard a rustle in the bushes—but decided to ignore it—you'd get eaten. The survivors, us, are hard-wired to attend to change.

So capture attention with variety. Otherwise, your audience will climb the wall, with or without a ladder.

But what if you don't want to be different?

Get Comfortable with Uncomfortable

"What you're asking us to do," the engineers told me, "won't work."

I was pushing them to spice up their presentations with a few techniques, such as moving away from the podium.

"Not comfortable," they said.

I know the feeling, so do you. It's how you feel every time you leave your comfort zone to learn something new.

The other day, for example, I purchased a new video camera for professional use. I didn't want to buy it. The old machine worked just fine, but the new machine, with newer technology, was better for my clients.

Still, I was resistant. "My problem," I told the Best Buy salesperson, "is that I really love the old machine. It's like a friend."

"I understand," she said, as if she too often grieved for machines. "But I think you'll be ok."

Have you ever learned a new skill that didn't, at first, feel uncomfortable? Remember your first bike ride? There you were, pedaling up the learning curve, feeling unnatural until, one day, you didn't.

Feeling unnatural is perfectly natural. And it doesn't mean there's anything wrong with you—or your bike.

"We can't ever leave the podium," the engineers said. "Or we'll die."

Well, ok, what they really said was that everyone used the podium—*that's the way presentations are done*—and these engineers wanted to look just like everyone else.

That's a problem, because if you look and sound like everyone else, you lose audience attention. Instead, when you stand up, stand out. You've got more chance of dying, or putting your audience to sleep, behind the podium than away from it.

Still, it doesn't feel that way.

These days, my old video camera sits at home, safely on the shelf. Sometimes I miss it. But I'm getting used to the new one, just as the engineers, I hope, are getting used to some new techniques.

That's what learning requires. Remember: there's nothing wrong with the bike. Keep pedaling.

Vary Your Enthusiasm

Sometimes being different means simply to vary your style. For example:

"Thanks for your reply!" an associate emailed me, with a cheerful exclamation point.

How many emails do you get, or send, that end like that? I get a lot! And I send them too! I think it's contagious!

But I don't end every email with an exclamation. It would be tiresome. Often, a low-key *thanks*, is perfectly fine. The email I got today—"Thanks for your reply!"—made it sound like my reply, or any reply at all, was downright amazing.

You can't sustain this level of astonishment. Nor would your colleagues want you to. A little goes a long way.

Same thing when speaking. You need to project energy, but that doesn't mean nonstop, hyper-caffeinated pep.

You project energy with physical variety—you gesture or move, then you're still. With visual variety—you show a PowerPoint slide, then darken the screen. With vocal variety—you talk, then ask a question, or you speak fast, then slow.

Energy comes from variety.

p.s. Ever wonder where the exclamation point came from? Probably not, but just in case: The Latin word *io* means *joy*, and "the Medieval copyists used to write *io* at the end of a sentence . . . [over time] the *i* moved above the *o*, and the *o* became smaller, becoming a point."

Thanks Wikipedia!

Speed Up/Slow Down

If you exercise, you probably know something about interval training. You get a better workout, fitness experts say, if you vary your pace.

For example, run, then walk, then sprint. Then keel over.

But when I do intervals, usually on the treadmill in our basement, it's for a different reason: to break monotony. Moving at a constant pace gets extremely boring. But if you change it up every few minutes, suddenly it's just moderately boring.

Let's apply this speed up/slow down principle to your communications.

1. **Writing**: Long sentences are good, but they slow things down, even if you use a dash or two—who doesn't love dashes? I certainly do—because, let's face it, a long sentence feels more like a marathon than a dash.

   Use short sentences too.

   It's the rhythm, back and forth, back and forth, that works.

2. **Speaking**: Do you naturally speak fast or slow?

   You're probably fast if, in your opinion, others speak so slowly that you need to frequently interrupt them and complete their sentences. You're probably slow if you're the one being interrupted.

   If you're naturally fast, pausing is your best friend.

   But pausing is a powerful tool for anyone. Pause for a second or two at the beginning of a presentation, before saying a word. That'll get attention. And pause, occasionally, before a key word or a key point.

   If your rhythm is slower, speed up. One good place: when telling your audience about the agenda. Let's suppose your agenda is about nutrition.

   "First," you say, "we'll discuss breakfast." (Now speed up.) "Is it really the most important meal of the day? Who says? And which is better: eggs, a granola bar, or Greek yogurt? Or should you just put them all in a smoothie, throw in a little kale, and be done with it? (Pause.) Then, we'll briefly discuss snacks . . ."

You can go fast while outlining your agenda—most people in your audience won't remember it anyway—since the real point of an agenda is to preview the themes and assure everyone you've got a plan.

So whether you're on a treadmill, delivering a presentation, writing a report, or doing all these things at once, vary your pace.

Do You Talk Too Fast?

Here's my theory: most fast talkers think they're talking at just the right speed—it's everyone else who's . . . talking . . . too . . . slowly.

Fast talkers don't bother me, unless they're leaving a phone number on my voice mail. Sometimes people leave their messages at nice, normal speeds until they get to their phone numbers—then they sprint!

They can't get the numbers out fast enough—are they trying to qualify for an Olympic event? It's as though they've got to yell 10 digits in under two seconds just to get into the race.

They might as well leave a message like this:

"You can reach me at number-number-number, I'm going to say these numbers so fast you'll never be able to call me back, ever, don't even try to decode it, you could play this message back 100 times, and even if you were able to identify the digits, which you won't, it still wouldn't matter because I'm really just shouting out 10 numbers at random, it's not even my phone number, I don't even know my phone number, it's more likely to be my Social Security number, or the bar code on the box of Cheerios, or your phone number. Have a nice day."

A good practice, whether you're talking in person or by phone, is to adapt to your audience. With voice mail, that means listening to the other person's outbound message, especially the speed, and then responding in kind.

Except for your phone number.[1]

Use Three Different Ways to Persuade: Head, Heart, Hands

There were 10 men in the room. All of us were stunned.

It was the last night of childbirth class. Up until then, we'd discussed childbirth rather extensively. Still, we had no idea, really, what to expect.

Childbirth, for the men, was an intriguing, faraway concept, sort of like New Zealand.

Then, last class, we watched a video. It showed a woman giving birth.

I wouldn't have minded some editing, here and there. But this video was determined to show everything, even if it took several days.

"That was unbelievable," one man said during the break.

"I'm not feeling well," said another.

No one, of course, had learned any new information. But something had changed.

You can know something in different ways. You can know, theoretically, that you're going to die. But that's different than knowing your death is imminent.

How then do you persuade others?

Sometimes, we assume that all it takes is the right information, or the right argument, to make a compelling case.

Wrong.

People are multi-dimensional. Imagine three centers of intelligence: head, heart, hands. Each requires something different.

1. **Head:** What do you want your audience to think? To influence thinking, provide facts and data. Use logic. Ask thought-provoking questions.

2. **Heart:** What do you want others to feel? To influence feeling, tell compelling stories. Ask others to imagine a vivid scene. Disclose how you feel.

3. **Hands:** What do you want others to do? To influence doing, model the desired behavior, or show what not to do. Encourage practice. Call for action.

I remember working with a jet engine company. If you make jet engines and you hear about a plane crash, the first thing you wonder is, *Was that one of our engines?*

One day the answer was yes. Fortunately, everyone on board survived, but the company seized the event as a teachable moment.

They invited the pilot into the plant. He showed pictures of his wife and children, he described how he felt as the plane was going down.

Everyone at the plant had always known about quality. But that pilot, that day, changed their commitment to quality.

The next time you communicate, consider head, heart, hands. When your message is important, speak to all three.

CHAPTER 6

The Easiest Way to Explain Anything

"Analogies . . . make one feel more at home."

—SIGMUND FREUD

Is Your Info Hard to Understand or to Picture? Try an Analogy

Let's say you're explaining something complicated, like the brain, to someone like me, whom you suspect may not have one.

Use an analogy.

The brain, you might say, is like a sponge (absorbs everything). Or a sieve (retains nothing). Or mush (seems to lack coherence).

You can easily picture a sponge, a sieve, or mush. A picture is no small thing. Most business info is abstract and hard to picture.

If your audience can't *visualize* what you're saying, they're more likely to daydream. Daydreams are visual. For example, *imagine being at the beach*. Notice you can *see* the beach.

Analogies are visual too. (So are stories, plus other techniques that we'll discuss shortly; please see sidebar on next page.)

We use analogies all the time, almost without thinking. Let's say you go to a French restaurant, and your companion has never eaten frog's legs. "Oh," you say, "tastes just like chicken."

An analogy is simply a comparison. *Frog's legs are like chicken.* You explain the *unknown, hard-to-picture X* (e.g., frog's legs) in terms of the *known, easy-to-picture Y* (chicken).

A lot of food tastes just like chicken. Often, that's because it *is* chicken. The main purpose of chicken, I believe, is to explain every other food.

Give your audience a picture:

1. Analogies

2. Stories: page 59

3. Show vs. tell: page 99

4. Talking about food: page 105

Trying to Explain Your Job? Use an Analogy

Ever try to explain your job to someone outside your field? It's almost impossible. Except for a few jobs on TV—doctor, lawyer, psychopath—no one really gets what anyone else does all day.

Your explanation sounds like this:

You: "I'm a technical, technical, technical. And what that means, basically, is that you'll never understand my job. No one does. Most days, I don't even understand it. My spouse has given up trying. She just tells people I'm a dental hygienist."

Other person (trying to be polite): "Your job sounds very interesting."

Here's the problem: they can't picture it. There are 12,000 occupations. Most are specialized and outside of everyday experience.

Solution? Use an analogy. Compare your complicated, hard-to-picture job with something that's easy-to-picture.

For example:

➡ "I'm like a weatherman who has to predict the financial

climate. I tell people that, sooner or later, it's going to rain. I just have no idea when." (Economic forecaster)

➡ "I'm like a lion tamer, except that I work with people." (Executive coach)

➡ "I'm a psychiatrist for machines. Everyone calls me when their computer acts weird." (IT support)

True, they still won't remember most of what you say. But they'll probably remember the image, and that means they'll probably remember you.

So what's your job like? Look for an image.

As for me: "I'm like a Brink's truck. I help business leaders deliver risky messages."

If, later today, you meet three other consultants who talk about biz communication, I'm betting that tomorrow, you'll remember the truck.

Use an Analogy to Avoid the "Curse of Knowledge"

The more you know about something, the worse you are at explaining it.

That's called the "curse of knowledge."[1] You forget what it's like to start from zero, not knowing anything.

Suppose, for example, you had to explain the Internet to someone who'd been living in a cave. How would you do it?

"The Internet," explains Wikipedia, "is the global system of interconnected computer networks that use the Internet protocol suite (TCP/IP) to link billions of devices worldwide."

You have to admit, that's amazing. The Internet, a complicated concept, is being explained by an even more complicated version of itself (the Internet protocol suite)—plus two acronyms (TCP/IP). You can smell the curse of knowledge.

Let's try an analogy.

The Internet, I'd say, is like a library—it's the best, worst, and strangest library ever imagined. (If we go back to chapter 2, *library* is the main message; *best*, *worst*, and *strangest* are three key points.)

Best library: You can get information about anything and everything, delivered in seconds to your own handheld gadget. And you can communicate with other users anywhere in the world.

Worst library: It's indifferent to whether content is true or false, useful or vile.

Strangest library: There's no mailing address, no building, no librarian. Where is it? The library doesn't exist in a physical location, but in a twilight-zone non-location called cyberspace, which basically means "we have no idea."

CHAPTER 7

Stories:
The 2.5 Step Method™

"Somebody gets into trouble, gets out of it again. People love that story. They never get sick of it."

—KURT VONNEGUT, author of 14 novels[1]

"Stories constitute the single most powerful weapon in a leader's arsenal."

—DR. HOWARD GARDNER, professor, Harvard University

Lose Your List, Tell a Story

I love lists as much as the next person. For example (and it's a list):

➡ Top 10 lists, such as the "Top 10 Most Dangerous Jobs." The most dangerous job, according to the Bureau of Labor Statistics: logging. (Good to know. Let's say you're working in an office, feeling time-pressured and stressed-out. Sure, you've got worries. But at least gigantic trees aren't falling on your head.)

➡ To Do lists: I use them daily, even weekends. Sometimes I put an item on the list that I have no likelihood, really, of ever doing. But writing it down makes me feel better.

➡ Angie's List: online service if you need an electrician, plumber, or logger. Finding an electrician is on my To Do list. I'm sure I'll be doing that very soon.

And there are lists in this book, including "The 10 Laws of Humor" on page 66.

But lists have their limits. Main problem: you've got to see the list to remember it. If I put "olives" on my shopping list, and then lose the list, there go the olives.

And if you're trying to influence or inspire others, showing them a list—for example, a bulleted list on a PowerPoint slide—is probably the worst way to do it.

Napoleon needed to inspire his soldiers to man an artillery battery under deadly fire. No one wanted to do it.

So Napoleon put up a large sign at the battery. He didn't list the "Top 10 Reasons to Volunteer for a Suicide Mission."

Instead, he wrote seven words: "The Battery of the Men without Fear."[2]

Step One for Creating a Story: Open with a Problem

Imagine you're speaking to a biz audience and want to get their attention with a quick story. Which opening line do you prefer?

1. "After a lot of unsuccessful interviews, I finally found work."
2. "After 10 years in prison, I feared that I'd never find another job in organized crime."

You may be thinking, "I dislike both. Too negative!" We'll come back to that objection in a second.

I like #2 for one simple reason: mystery. We don't know how this story turns out. Opening #1, by contrast, reveals everything.

Years ago, I went to a writing workshop led by the head writer of a well-known sitcom that I'd never heard of.

"My job," the head writer said, "is ridiculously easy. Every week, the writers pitch ideas for future episodes. I'm the one who decides whether to develop an idea or kill it.

"I've only got one criterion," she said. "Do I care what happens next? If I do, we develop the story; if not, we bury it."

Let's go back to the "negative" objection. Being negative, opening with a problem, is a plus. Problems hook an audience.

Later in the story, the problems need to be resolved. And if it's a business audience, you also need to deliver a compelling point. But that's later.

Think about it. Every story, and life too, is about problems and obstacles, and "what happens next."

Going to see a movie? Suppose it's a traditional romantic comedy, because you're not in the mood for anything heavy.

Still, there'll be plenty of problems.

The story will never be: Boy meets girl, they fall instantly in love, have a beautiful wedding, then pursue brilliant careers, raise gifted children, win the lottery, and live happily ever after.

No one's making that movie. No one wants to see that movie. There's no story.

Instead, you'll see: Boy meets girl, they fall in love, then boy does something incredibly stupid. Girl says, "That's it, we're done." Boy feels despondent, tries everything to win her back, finally does, and then does something even stupider . . .

For some reason, it's always the boy who screws everything up.

But that's another story.

p.s. I'm at the airport bookstore, flipping through books, reading first lines.

Best opening: "First, I'll tell about the robbery our parents committed. Then about the murders, which happened later."[3]

Problem, problem, problem.

Experiment with Different Openings

Here are seven different openings to a story, based on a single problem I experienced:

1. "Do you think he has a gun?" I asked my friend.

   It was past midnight. We had driven to an isolated place where a big muscular guy was waiting for me. He wanted money.

"This guy doesn't need a gun," my friend said. "He could kill us with his bare hands."

(You don't need to open with the very first thing that happened. Here, we begin in the middle.)

2. (Same story, different opening.) I knew I was in trouble when my friend drove off. It was the middle of night, in the middle of nowhere.

"Come back," I yelled. "I have no money."

(Remember, this is just the opening. The next few lines would explain the context.)

3. "Every night, 20 new people hate my guts," the big muscular guy said. "On a good night, 30 people." Then he spit. "I could care less."

(You can also start with a character.)

4. "A few hours ago," the big muscular guy told me, "we watched you get out of your car, leave the parking lot, and walk down the street. That was your mistake. You should have never done that."

(Once again, we're starting in the middle.)

5. "It's your own fault," my mother said. "I would have never parked there."

(It's ok to embellish. My mother, for example, never said this. But she might have.)

6. When I returned to the parking lot after dinner, my car had vanished.

(This is the first thing that actually happened.)

7. "Apparently, you can't read," the big muscular guy said. "Otherwise you would have seen the sign in the parking lot: If you walk off the premises, your car will be towed."

(Think about what you want to reveal in the opening, and what you want to leave out. I wouldn't use this last opening—it reveals too much.)

p.s. The tow guy demanded cash ($112) for my car. My friend, who had driven off, came back and took me to an ATM.

Step Two: Close Your Story with a Business-Relevant Point

Midnight in Boston, I have a near-death experience.

Just back from a business trip, I'm getting my car from Logan airport. Unfortunately, I parked on the roof of the garage. It's been snowing, so I need to do some scraping, and brushing, and muttering.

The roof is not good. It's like parking your car on the top of your house.

When you exit the roof, you drive down a one-way spiral ramp—round and round you go!—like a very intense amusement ride.

Suddenly, out of nowhere, a car appears. It's going the wrong way, toward me.

Let's pause for a moment. Sooner or later, this story is going to need a point, especially for a business audience. And the longer the build-up, the stronger the point better be.

Back at Logan, the wrong-way car misses me by inches. We both keep driving into the night.

Ok, you're thinking, so what?

"My point is X," you say at the end of your story.

Here's where you decide, similar to your life, what things mean. And things mean whatever you say they mean—at least in a story.

Take this story. What's the X?

➡ "People are idiots."

No, no, no. That's a terrible point, especially if you're talking to a room full of people. And even if true, what's your audience supposed to do?

X should be a call to action.

➡ "When you exit Logan from the roof, be prepared for anything."

Well, if someone's unfamiliar with Boston, that X might be helpful. But it's extremely literal. The story never leaves the garage.

Create a bigger meaning.

➡ "Get feedback."

For this X to work, ask your audience, metaphorically, "Ever go the wrong way?"

Now, you're no longer talking about airport parking; you're talking about work, and about life, and this is now a story about feedback.

"Maybe," you say, "the people around you are honking their horns and cursing you out. But you're oblivious. Get some feedback, for god's sake, before it's too late."

➡ "Stop blaming people. Find the root cause."

Suppose the audience, like me, blames the other driver. Ok, throw in a twist: maybe that driver made a wrong turn because of a confusing sign. Maybe he's not the problem at all.

Maybe there's something terribly wrong with this entire garage.

Apart from the roof . . .

When speaking to a business audience, you need a compelling point. A good story has multiple points, which means you can refashion it for different audiences and different purposes.

But each time you tell it, stick to one point.

Step 2.5: Move from the First Line to the Last, Quickly

Sometimes you hear stories that go like this: "Last Thursday—no wait, I think it was Wednesday.

"Oh, I just remembered where I was Wednesday—Cincinnati, it was a last-minute business trip, which happens all the time at our company. Can't anyone plan ahead?—so it definitely wasn't Wednesday.

"Actually, I'm not sure this thing that I'm about to tell you really even happened. I think I might have dreamt it. Last Thursday . . ."

No one cares about Wednesday or Thursday. They care how long your story takes.

Edit.

Let's Put This Together: Use My 2.5 Step Method™

A story is a mini-presentation; it's got an opening (first line), middle, and end (last line).

1. (Opening) Create a first line that grabs attention and makes your audience wonder, *What happened next?*
2. (End) Create a last line that inspires business-relevant action.
3. (Middle) Connect the dots, first line to last, quickly. Often, that means cutting everything in the middle by ½.

Here's an example:

"After only two days of marriage," the man began. But before he could continue, I interrupted. (I was leading a workshop, *When Leaders Speak*, and we were practicing first and last lines.)

Your story, I said, can go in one of two directions:

1. The good place, for example, "After only two days of marriage, I was more in love than I ever dreamt possible."
2. The other place.

I polled the audience of 100+ people for their preference. No one was especially interested in the good place.

"After only two days," the man continued, "I no longer recognized my wife."

Bingo! He had us. And yes, there was definitely a problem here, but, remember, that's what a story is. A good story hooks us with a bad problem.

The positive part comes later with the resolution, what the storyteller learned through experience, and what we learn by listening.

In the marriage story, the middle (which we never heard) would explain why he no longer recognized his wife.

Did he have a change of heart? Or maybe he couldn't recognize her, literally, due to sudden amnesia—perhaps caused by a blow to the head delivered by the wife who, he discovered after only two days, was occasionally homicidal.

(Probably better, in this story, to talk more about his flaws than his wife's. The first will make him likable, the second won't.)

How does his marriage story end? "Stick to the plan," he told us.

"Stick to the plan" is a call to action, relevant to any business audience, regardless of marital status. He uses the example of marriage to make a point about work: commit.

And he's a credible messenger; the story makes him credible. And it makes us, the audience, pay attention.

p.s. Wondering how his marriage turned out? So far, so good, he reports—now, 16 years later.

What about a "Funny" Story? Follow the 10 Laws of Humor

1. **Never say, "I've got a funny story."** Business humor (most humor, really) should be unexpected. Plus, don't overpromise.

   Promise "funny," and your audience may resist you. It's as if they're thinking, "Ok, funny guy, go ahead, make us laugh."

   Just tell your story.

2. **Be concise.** You already know the value of getting to the point. Double that for humor.

   A joke has two parts: setup, punch line. Consider Henny Youngman's, "Take my wife. Please." The setup is three words, the punch line, one.

   The longer your setup, the stronger your punch line needs to be. Stay short.

3. **Pause.** Your delivery and timing matter in any presentation.

   If you say, "Take my wife (or my husband, or my roommate, or my cellmate). Please," you've got to pause before the word *please*, or it doesn't work.

   Don't rush. Take your time.

4. **Don't tell stale jokes.** "Did you hear the one about the Democrat, the Republican, and the zookeeper . . . ?" Sounds formulaic. Your audience will groan.

Humor should be original. And, if you're speaking to a business audience, it should have a business-relevant point.

5. Don't target other groups or individuals. Unless you're trying to be unlikable.

The next four are about specific techniques, with examples from my published work in newspapers and books.

6. Be self-deprecating. Suppose, for example, you're talking about long-range career planning, 5–10 years out, and how it's admirable but hard to do:

"I read that a former CEO of Coca-Cola set the goal of becoming CEO 10 years before it happened. According to *Fortune*, he even set a target date that turned out to be remarkably close.

"Stories like this always make me feel worse. I will probably never become the CEO of Coke. Even if I plan ahead and write it on my 10-year goal list: COKE!

"For one thing, I don't have a 10-year goal list. This is something I should have thought about 10 years ago."[4]

7. Exaggerate. Let's say the subject is technology and how fast it changes:

"Our old computer sits alone in the basement now. It's nearly five years old. That's human years. A computer year is less than a minute, so by the time you get one home and out of the box, it's more than 100 years old.

"That's why the store won't take it back, unless you also return the box and all the packing materials. Never underestimate the resale value of packing materials."[5]

8. Think opposites. For example, consider worry. Many of us worry too much; we already know that. So take the opposite tack:

"All this 'Don't worry, be happy' talk makes me nervous. It's important to worry frequently and vigorously. Worry exercises the imagination . . . For me, worrying is the perfect hobby, if you want to relax."[6]

9. **Use the rule of three.** In a list with three items, the first two establish a pattern, the third breaks the pattern and surprises.

   "I have this recurrent dream where I'm an important leader. Sometimes I'm a Fortune 500 CEO, sometimes a big city mayor, sometimes a highly respected chimpanzee. And all the employees, citizens, and monkeys give me their labor, their votes, and their bananas."[7]

10. **Don't try too hard to be funny.** Your goal is to engage your audience. Humor is simply a tool, one of many.

    So, at best, go for a smile. You're probably not a comic. And you don't want to become a joke.

CHAPTER 8

Vary from Announce to Discuss

"When you run General Electric, there are 7 to 12 times a year when you have to say, 'you're doing it my way.' If you do it 18 times, the good people will leave. If you do it 3 times, the company falls apart."

—JEFFREY IMMELT,
CEO, General Electric[1]

"I like to do all the talking myself. It saves time, and prevents arguments."

—OSCAR WILDE,
playwright

When You Make an Announcement, Be Clear: This Decision Is Nonnegotiable

Some of us are confused, both at work and at home, about which decisions are open for debate and which aren't. The first is a discussion; the second, an announcement.

When my son was little, he often heard everything I said as a discussion. The statement "Go to bed right now—before I call the POLICE!" was, for my son, simply an opening gambit.

Announcements are different from discussions; they should look, sound, and feel different.[2] As a leader, it's easy to get tripped up; you might overuse one mode or send out confusing signals about which mode you're in.

69

Firing someone is an announcement. You wouldn't say, "George, suppose, just for argument's sake, we asked you to turn in your badge, pack up your desk, and get the hell out of here—would that be terribly inconvenient?"

One night, I told my son, in no uncertain terms, to go upstairs and brush his teeth. I thought it was an announcement. But he stood his ground: "You are not the boss of me," he said.

"Who is the boss of you?" I wondered. Maybe I could call that person for advice.

And yet, I wasn't overly concerned. Bedtime struggles, I figured, fell into the category of problems that solve themselves. This issue would disappear with age and maturity.

My wife was dubious: "Age and maturity? How much older do you need to be?" The problem, she implied in a very subtle *Why are you not getting this, you idiot?* sort of way, was with me. I needed to be more of a boss.

Fair enough. And so, as I aged and matured, I grew more comfortable with authority. Eventually, I was able to get my son to bed without even mentioning the police . . .

Whether you announce or discuss, be clear which one you're doing. (For more, please see *Command*, page 146.)

When You Make an Announcement, Explain the "Why"

To build trust, it's not enough to announce what you're doing, even if what you're doing is right. You need to explain why it's right. For example:

8:30 a.m. My wife and I park our car, carry our bikes onto a "bike bus," and hang them from ceiling hooks. The bus goes to the Martha's Vineyard ferry, which leaves soon, at 9:30 a.m.

The bus driver looks unhappy about having actual passengers. "I won't be departing till 9:10," she announces. Her tone implies, "Don't get your hopes up. Life is disappointing."

By 8:50, the bus is full of restless passengers and dangling bikes. "Why are we leaving so late?" asks a passenger.

"Because I've been doing this job for 12 years and that's when we're leaving," the driver says. In other words, *Don't question my authority.*

"How long does it take to get to the dock?" I ask.

The bus driver looks at my wife: "Tell your husband to relax. We'll be there by 9:17—trust me."

Ok. But that only leaves 13 minutes to remove a busload of bikes and luggage, buy ferry tickets, and board the boat.

For this plan to work, everyone will need to be extremely caffeinated. I wonder if there's any way, in the next few minutes, for each passenger to drink at least 10–20 cups of coffee.

The bus gets quiet as we wait. "I'm surprised there's not more conversation," the bus driver says.

"We're afraid of you," says a passenger.

9:10 a.m. We're off! The bus barrels down the narrow road at breakneck speed. The bikes swing recklessly from above, luggage flies off the rack, passengers cling to their seats.

It's the most exciting bus ride I've ever been on!

"Don't they have any speed limits in the U.S.?" gasps a Canadian woman who's bouncing up and down next to us.

"This whole trip is stupid," says her friend. "I just want to go home."

At 9:17 a.m., we arrive at the dock. Thirteen minutes later, we're on the ferry. The bus driver, it turns out, was right about the math. But wrong about expecting us to trust her.

Maybe there was a good reason for the 9:10 departure. Maybe she knew the ferry would wait, no matter when we arrived. But why not say that?

"I'll never get on a bus with that driver again," says the Canadian woman.

"I just want to go home," says her friend.

To Increase Your Influence, Give Away Some Control

On my way home from work, my wife sometimes phones: "Is there any way you could possibly pick up some milk?" she asks.

I know right away that I'm headed for the supermarket. But my wife has a sweet way of asking—she gives me the illusion of control. I don't even drink milk, but I support the concept.

No one likes being told what to do, so people who are skilled influencers avoid overusing the announcement or "tell" mode.

On the other hand, suppose you've made a nonnegotiable decision: "We need vast quantities of low fat, farm fresh milk in this house right away!"

Well, most decisions are multi-dimensional: there's a *what, how, when, where,* and *who.* Can you find somewhere to flex?

Recently, for example, I was working with a manager who needed to send someone to a client meeting in North Dakota. It was winter, North Dakota was cold. No one wanted to go.

The manager knew the *what* (meet client), *how* (face-to-face), and *where* (North Dakota). Those things were nonnegotiable, but everything else was flexible. She really didn't care *who* went, or *when,* whether this week or next.

So she threw the problem out to her staff and let them decide. They decided to draw straws after work, over a drink.

Probably not milk.

When Discussing a Problem, Let the Other Person Talk First

My wife and I were having dinner at a Boston seafood restaurant that we like a lot, for the main reason that we've never had a bad meal there, or been poisoned.

I ordered fisherman's stew and immediately felt buyer's remorse, although I appreciate the idea of being a fisherman. My wife ordered grilled shrimp and a baked potato.

Time passed. The waitress stopped by for a visit and to "explain the story about what happened to your dinner." Sounded ominous. Still, I enjoy a good story as much as the next fisherman.

"Your fisherman's stew has been ready for some time," she said, "but someone stole the grilled shrimp for another table." Not good news. I was especially discouraged about the stew: Was there something wrong with it? How come no one wanted to steal it?

More time passed. When the food arrived, the baked potato was cold, and the broth from the stew had evaporated or, I could only hope, been stolen.

A manager stopped by to check on things. We told her the story about dinner. She looked sad.

"What would you like me to do?" she asked.

We didn't have anything particular in mind.

"All right," she said. "How about we pay for your dinner?"

We didn't argue. She still looked sad.

"Also, I'm also going to wrap up two complimentary desserts—pumpkin cheesecake and Boston cream pie."

Completely unnecessary, we said. But we accepted the gift anyway, in the interest of cheering her up . . .

The next time you talk to someone about a problem, don't be too fast to offer, or insist on, your solution. While it's good to have some suggestions in mind, try letting the other person go first.

p.s. If possible, avoid fisherman's stew. Substitute pumpkin cheesecake.

- -

Announce or Discuss?

Announce when:

- The matter is nonnegotiable (due to laws, safety concerns, company policies, etc.).
- It's an emergency—there's no time to discuss.
- You have expertise, others don't.

Discuss when:

- You need the buy-in of others.
- The matter is more important to others than to you.
- Others have as much knowledge and experience as you do. Or their complete lack of experience gives them a fresh perspective.

And you have more than two options.

Imagine, for example, you're a military commander. Consider these options (they go from more control to less):

1. Announce (high control): "We need to take the hill! Now!"

2. Announce, plus explain "why": "We need to take the hill now. Because otherwise, we're all going to DIE."

3. Announce the goal, but discuss the means (moderate control): "We need to take the hill now. What's the best way to do that?"

4. Discuss others' ideas, and then you decide: "I think we should take the hill. But I'd like to hear other suggestions before I decide."

5. Discuss others' ideas, and then they decide (low control): "How would you like to spend the afternoon? I suppose we could take the hill. But it's really up to you . . ."

If you're going to discuss, you need to ask smart questions. That's next.

CHAPTER 9

Questions:
How to Ask the Best—and
Answer the Worst

"My greatest strength as a consultant is to be ignorant and ask a few questions."

—PETER DRUCKER,
management consultant, author of 39 books

"Management teams aren't good at asking questions. In business school, we train them to be good at giving answers."

—CLAYTON CHRISTENSEN,
professor, Harvard Business School

Find Your Balance between Making Assertions and Asking Questions

When Kevin Sharer became CEO of Amgen, a $14 billion biotech company, he spent 150 hours asking questions.

150 hours. He interviewed 150 Amgen leaders, one hour each.

Would you have done that?

Smart people ask smart questions, although this isn't always easy. I remember preparing a roomful of executives at a Fortune 100 company for a Q & A session with their company's new chairman. They didn't want to ask anything, nor did they want to be asked anything.

"Anything we say could be extremely career-limiting," they explained.

Then the chairman walked into the room. He immediately stripped off his jacket and tie, as if to say, "I'm a regular guy." Then he sat down and, after a few minutes, everyone relaxed, probably because he didn't undress further.

When you ask a skillful question, you raise the IQ of the room, and you stand out—it's another 8-second moment.

Kevin Sharer asked five main questions, such as: "what are three things you want to change?" and "what are three things you want to keep?"[1]

Note the specific number, three things, which pushes the other person to get specific (please also see page 85, *Push for Specifics.*).

Question: Are you more comfortable asking questions or providing answers? Be known as someone who does both.

Before Giving Advice, Ask a Few Questions

"I think the main reason you employ me," Bob said, "is to hear yourself talk."

Bob was a career strategist who'd run the career office at Harvard before opening a private practice.

I sometimes consulted him for advice. Except that he hardly gave any. His role, as he saw it, wasn't to tell me what to do. It was to engage in dialogue so that I could figure things out myself. But the dialogue was crucial.

How often do you give advice?

Advice isn't bad. When you have expertise, and the other person doesn't, your advice may be useful. I give lots of advice when coaching executives on leadership messages or presentations. Advice is what they expect and value.

But sometimes, when someone wants you to solve their problem, it's better not to.

The downside of advice? It robs others of the chance to develop judgment.

When people ask me for advice, I often listen for a while, then ask a question like this: "Suppose you were talking to a very wise person. What would she or he advise you to do?"

"She'd advise me to stay put," said a colleague. He'd been wrestling with whether to accept a job at another company. Suddenly, he knew the answer.

A similar question: "What would Person X do (where X is a role model)?"

Movie director Steven Spielberg, while making *Jaws*, struggled with a mechanical shark that didn't work. He could have called Alfred Hitchcock for advice. Instead, he asked himself, *What would Hitchcock do?*

Answer: Don't show the shark. It's scarier.

It's scarier to let people solve problems on their own. It's easier just to give an answer.

But the next time someone knocks on your door for advice, remember: that's a coachable moment.

Sharpen Your Questions

"Do you like horror movies?"

You're probably not asking this question at work—it's from an online dating service, OkCupid—unless your company is a nightmare, and you need to warn others.

JOB APPLICANT: This seems like a good place to work. Is it?
YOU: That depends. Do you like horror movies?

But the horror movie question is instructive if you want to sharpen your questions.

1. Open vs. closed: The first thing you notice is that it's closed, meaning you'll get a one-word, yes/no response.

Q: Are closed questions bad? (A closed question.)
A: No.
Q: So why do we care about the open/closed distinction? (An open question.)
A: Because closed questions limit the info you get. And limit the other person's engagement.

Q: What % of questions at work are closed? (Closed.)

A: 82.6%.

Q: Where did you get that figure? (Open.)

A: I just made it up. But at your next business meeting, keep score. You'll be surprised by the tilt.

FYI: Even if you already know the open/closed distinction, common knowledge is not common practice. Do you ask too many closed questions? (Closed.) Check.

2. Your inferences: OkCupid discovered that if two people, now dating, gave the same answer to certain questions (in an initial survey), their odds of having a long-term relationship went up.

OkCupid identified three significant questions (listed on page 79), not just one. And even then, the correlation was only 32%.

FYI: Be careful what you infer from any one answer.

3. A questioning strategy: Sometimes you need a series of questions, deliberately sequenced. For example:

Q: Do you like horror movies? (Closed.)

A: No.

Q: How would you feel about dating someone who loved horror movies? (Open.)

A: Afraid.

Q: Because you might have to sit through a lot of blood and gore? (Closed.)

A: No, because I'm already married.

Q: Ok, but suppose you were single. Would the horror movie difference be a deal-breaker? (Closed.)

A: No.

Q: What differences would be deal-breakers? (Open. And the key question in this sequence.)

FYI: Plan your questioning strategy. Resist the temptation to just wing it.

p.s. The three OkCupid questions (and my answers, which match my wife's):

1. Do you like horror movies? No.
2. Have you ever traveled around a foreign country alone? Yes. (Warning: Don't ask your date this question, lest she assume that being with you will feel like going somewhere strange, and then being abandoned.)
3. Wouldn't it be fun to chuck it all and go live on a sailboat? No. (I don't love sailboats, so this idea sounds a lot like a horror movie.)

Not All Open Questions Are Smart

A smart question gets others to think. Most ordinary questions, whether open or closed, don't do that — nor is there any reason they should, if it's a casual conversation.

Consider these questions about the "weekend."

1. "Did you have a good weekend?" you ask a colleague. Typical question, and it's closed.

2. "How was your weekend?" Technically an open question, but you'll often get a one-word response ("good").

3. "What did you do over the weekend?" Open, but you won't spark any new thinking.

Again, all three questions are perfectly fine. No one's looking for deep insights about the weekend.

But suppose you were?

4. "What would your ideal weekend look like?" This question is different; it makes the other person think.

Let's apply smart questions to work. Imagine you're a manager, talking with one of your employees about his job satisfaction. You could ask, "How was your day?" or "How's it going?" but these questions won't take you far.

Try a variation of question #4:

"What would an ideal day at work look like for you?" Or, "Tell me about one of your best days here." And then, "How can we create more of those?"

Smart questions get others to think. But before you can ask one, you need to think.

Your Questioning Strategy: Start Low Risk

If you're asking multiple questions, begin with the easy ones. Let's say you're leading a senior executive meeting at your company to discuss the new corporate values, which don't seem to working. Your sequence of questions could look like this:

a. (Low risk): On a 1–10 scale, to what extent do our employees know the values? Asking a "1–10" question is a good start. The answer will rarely be a 1 or a 10; usually, you'll get a middle number, 4–8. But then you can ask the natural follow-up: "How can we get to a 9 or 10?"

b. (More risky): To what extent do employees believe the values? They may know the values, but not really buy into them. And the next question might explain why.

c. (Most risky): How, specifically, have we, the leaders, demonstrated the values?

You could also ask, "Who here knows the values?" But asking a group the "Who here knows about X" question—where X could be anything whatsoever—is always risky.

"Who here knows what to do if you're bitten by a rattlesnake?" is not a good question at a meeting, unless the meeting happens to involve hiking through rattlesnake-infested terrain, and one or more people just got bitten.

But at a normal meeting, someone might know a lot about X, but not raise his hand out of fear you'll call on him. Someone else might not know a thing about X, but raise his hand anyway, because everyone else has hands up.

No one wants to look stupid. What's the risk your question will do that?

p.s. From *Snakebite! What to Do If You're Bitten*: "It's important to get away from the snake as soon as possible so it does not bite again. Do not try to capture the snake."[2]

Hmm. Capturing the snake never even occurred to me.

Before Asking a Risky Question, Disclose Why You're Asking

Imagine these two scenarios.

Scenario #1: Sweat

The CEO of your company summons you to her office. "Is this a high-performing organization?" she asks.

You start to sweat. What's the best answer, you wonder, to keep your job?

Apart from scaring people, the question is flawed by its closed, yes-no form. It will yield little info. Yet one CEO called it her favorite question.

> **Better:** "In what ways is this a high-performing organization?" And then, "How could we improve?" Or ask for *three ways* the organization is high performing, and *three ways* it's not, similar to Kevin Sharer's approach (page 75).

> **Best:** Before asking anything, say why you're asking. For example: "I'm committed to making this a high-performing organization—I'm sure you are too—and that's a never-ending process. I'd love your perspective on what's working and what's not."

Scenario #2: No sweat

Her first week at a large insurance company, a young employee did something fearless. She called up the CEO and asked if she could stop by, because she wanted to get a feel for the company and where it was going.

Intrigued, the CEO said yes.

But her supervisor didn't know about the meeting till later. He was furious. "I've been at this company for over 10 years," he said. "I've never even met the CEO."

You could argue that the new hire was naive, that she didn't know about the chain of command, and that she won't ever do this again. Fine, but what's the cost to the organization?

The cost is fear.

Which scenario, #1 or #2, is more common in your organization?

Years ago, consultant Tom Peters popularized "management by walking around." He urged managers to get out of the office, ask questions, and find out what's really going on.

Great advice, except for one thing: Most people, unlike that new hire, are reluctant to speak truth to power.

Don't underestimate fear.

Before you ask a tough question, reduce the fear. Say why you're asking.

Avoid Asking Loaded Questions, at Least 95% of the Time

"Do you want to sell sugared water for the rest of your life?" Steve Jobs asked John Sculley, then president of PepsiCo. "Or do you want to come with me and change the world?"

That's a loaded question. It says, "Look, this job of yours, running PepsiCo, is extremely silly. I'm offering something big."

Sculley was persuaded it was big; he took the job as Apple's CEO. (Years later, he would call the job a big mistake.)

Do you ever ask loaded questions? Suppose you work at McDonald's. You might ask:

1. "Would you like fries with that order?" Perfectly reasonable. You're suggesting an option.
2. "You're going to want fries with that order, aren't you?" Ok, now you're getting pushy.
3. "You can get fries or a shake for half price—which do you want?" Even pushier—this is known in sales as an "assumptive close." You assume, aloud, they must want something.

I generally avoid questions like #2 or #3. Except for one time . . .

I'd gone to a job-hunting workshop in my 20s, led by a career expert who gave lots of tips, including, "If you're ever invited for an interview in a faraway city, make sure to ask the following question."

I wrote the question down in my notebook, although it seemed nervy. A few months later, a recruiter called about a job in Miami.

After we scheduled an interview, I put the recruiter on hold, dashed around the apartment, found the notebook, tore through the pages, got the question, and returned to the phone.

"Will you be sending the plane ticket," I asked, "or would you prefer me to invoice you?" (That's the "fries or shake" assumptive close.)

After a short pause, which seemed endless, the recruiter agreed to the invoice.

So I went to Miami. I didn't get the job, but not because of the question. Today, that question seems tame and, of course, worth asking.

Does that mean assumptive questions are ok? Well, it depends on the context. And that reminds me of something else the career expert said:

"For 95% of you, when you think you're being obnoxiously aggressive, you're really just being appropriately assertive."

Good advice. Unless you're in that 5%.

Go to the Dark Side

I call them *opposite questions.*

Try this one at your next team-building retreat: "Suppose our group wanted to win an award for being completely dysfunctional. What would we do?"

Sometimes people get tired of best practices. When that happens, flip the question and ask about the worst.

Taking a short detour gets people warmed up. You'll be surprised by how many answers you get and how energized people are.

If you ask the dysfunctional team question, people will say things like:

"We'd gossip, we'd text, we'd gossip and text. No wait, we already do all that."

Later, of course, you'll need to flip the question and discuss what you need to do more of, less of, or differently. For example, with the dysfunctional list, you'd ask, "Which of these items should we be most concerned about?"

Vary the opposite question, depending on topic:

Customer Service: "What are the 20 best ways to completely alienate our top clients?" This question is frightening—you may already be doing a few.

Stress: "How could we make working here so anxiety-provoking that you'd need an industrial strength horse tranquilizer just to walk through the door?"

Management: "Suppose you wanted to be the worst manager in the synthetic resin industry?" Hmm. Possible response: "I don't know a thing about the synthetic resin industry." (Ok, that's a good start!)

Turns out, it's easy to brainstorm worst practices. Most of us have had impressive experience.

Push for Specifics

"Tell me about your culture," you ask the hiring manager.

You're considering a new job, so you really need to know, because even the best job—in the worst culture—will kill your satisfaction and success.

But you've asked the wrong question. It's too abstract, too vague, and will prompt the other person to give you a bland answer.

Here's what you're likely (and unlikely) to hear:

- ➡ We're innovative. (The truth is, we have no idea what we're doing.)
- ➡ We embrace change. (Our priorities change from minute to minute.)
- ➡ Picture one big family. (Picture one big unhappy family.)
- ➡ We work hard. (We avoid frivolous activities like weekends.)
- ➡ Read our core values statement. It says it all. (Read the 207-page report the U.S. Dept. of Justice just issued. Our CEO has promised to turn things around. As he says, "Anyone can work from jail.")

"I hate the word culture," says the CEO of GM, Mary Barra. "It's like this thing that sits out there".[2]

What is culture, anyway?

"It's the stories we tell about the company," Barra says. "It's how we behave."

Agreed. So don't ask about culture. Ask about stories and behaviors, with questions like these:

Stories: "Tell me about someone who's been really successful here" (not just based on technical skill, but on modeling key values). "And tell me about someone who hasn't."

Behavior: "Suppose I exceeded my performance goals. What other factors would contribute to a high-performance rating here? What would get me a low-performance rating, even if I met objectives?"

For example, here's what the creator of Time Warner, Steve Ross, said about risk-taking behavior: "I'll never fire you for making a mistake. I'll fire you for not making any."[3]

It's a mistake to ask bland questions. Push for specifics . . .

At a job interview:

You're the interviewer, and you greet the job applicant in the lobby: "Did you have any trouble finding us?" you ask.

You've got two big interview questions, and this isn't one of them. This is filler. Filler questions break the ice.

But we also use fillers when we're unsure what to ask next and we're desperate to ask something.

Sometimes with a problem—any problem—we don't know *what* we need to learn, or, even if we know, we don't know *how* to learn it.

Consider the problem of hiring the right person:

- *What* do you need to learn about the applicant? Well, you need to learn whether he can do the job and also fit into the organization.
- *How* will you learn it? You need to ask the right questions. Unfortunately, the right questions don't just magically appear; you need to think them through in advance.

Suppose, as the interviewer, you begin indirectly: "Tell me about yourself," you ask, without broadcasting what, exactly, you're looking for.

Still, you do need to know what, exactly, you're looking for.

Lurking beneath your opener is one of your two big questions; you won't ask it directly, but it will drive most of your questions: WHY SHOULD WE HIRE YOU?

Let's shift to the job applicant and his response. "Well, I could talk about my marketing background, my leadership experience, or my last triathlon. Where should I start?"

Here, he's asked a smart counter question. He's given you fast, bulleted info, presented as options that say, "You should hire me because I've got X, Y, and Z." And he did it in 8 seconds.

(The triathlon, by the way, is not trivial—it shows energy, discipline, and achievement. Plus, it adds variety. Unlike marketing and leadership, it's personal.)

> *You:* "Let's talk marketing. Any experience with social media?"

Is social media experience a must-have? What, exactly, are you looking for?

> *Applicant:* "Yes! To launch our new office machine—a combo phone, fax, and microwave oven—we made a series of YouTube videos called 'Indestructible.'"

So far, the applicant is doing ok. Unfortunately, he's about to get worse.

> *You:* "Suppose your boss were sitting here. What kind of constructive feedback might she give you?"

Here's the other big question you're fishing for: WHY SHOULDN'T WE HIRE YOU? Asking about constructive feedback is one way to probe.

> *Applicant:* "Well, she'd say I'm aggressive."
>
> *You:* "In what way?"

When someone uses abstractions, like *aggressive*, don't pretend you understand. Aggressive could be good or bad. Ask for specific examples.

> *Applicant:* "For the YouTube campaign 'Indestructible,' my concept was to first spill coffee on the machine, then drop it on the floor, then hurl it out a window, and then take a sledgehammer and try to bludgeon the thing to death."
>
> *You:* "Ok. We'll get back to you . . ."
>
> Whether you're interviewing a job applicant, meeting a client, or coaching an employee, figure out what you really need to learn, and then how to ask.

Let's talk now about answering questions—nightmare or otherwise.

When Asked a Question, You Have Options— Use Them

Suppose you're giving a presentation:

1. **Answer the question.** Sure, if you know the answer. But no one expects you to know the answer to every question. And you'll lose credibility if you pretend you do.

2. **Ask the questioner a counter question.**
   a. Ask him to clarify: "Could you say a bit more about that?" Sometimes there's a more important question underneath the first one. Other times, you really have no idea what he's talking about—yikes!—until he says more.
   b. Ask her to answer: "I'm flattered you're asking me that, because I know you've thought a lot about this topic. How would you answer the question?" This works well when she really has some expertise and may be dying to talk.

3. **Defer.**
   a. For a few minutes: "We'll be covering that in about 20 minutes, please give me a shout if we haven't answered your question by then."

    b. Till the break: "I'd love to discuss that with you over coffee." Good move if the question will derail you and no one else in the audience is interested.

    c. Till the end of the day: "Let's put that on the parking lot." Then create a chart that says "Parking Lot," and make sure to actually do something with those items later.

    d. Till later that week: "I'd like to do some research on that. Would it be ok to get back to you in 48 hours?"

Let's linger on this option, it's a good one. Here's what you've just communicated (in *8 seconds*):

➡ You're a serious person, and you take the question seriously.

➡ You don't bluff.

➡ You keep your commitments (because, of course, you will follow up).

So your influence is actually enhanced—much more than if you tried to wing it.

    e. Till the end of time: This is appropriate for borderline questions, the ones where you wish an HR exec would suddenly appear and make a house arrest. Stay calm, stay friendly, and then move on (for more detail, please see page 91, *When the Question is Too Personal, Decline*).

4. Refer.

    a. Refer the question to the group at large: "Good question, what do we think about that?" Then move off stage to the side, while the group discusses it. Return to the center of the room when you're ready to summarize and resume control.

    b. Refer the question to a specific table group. Walk over to the group. Wait for their answer. Then take their answer to another table group, as if the first group's answer is the craziest thing you ever heard. Ask the second group what they think. Then take their answer back to the first group. Good for stimulating group discussion—and/or stirring up trouble.

5. **Bridge**.

    a. Find a keyword or key phrase in the question to dwell on for a moment, before you move the conversation back to your comfort zone. Politicians do this all the time—returning, over and over, to their talking points—but you should do it sparingly. Otherwise, you'll sound like a politician.

    b. Answer the question beneath the one that was asked—the question you're comfortable with. "I think what you're really asking is . . ."

An Example of the Bridge Technique

As a warm-up exercise in one of my workshops, I sometimes ask participants to talk for a minute, in pairs, about a ridiculous topic. For example, I ask them to speak about "sports played on the planet Jupiter," while agreeing with the crazy premise that Jupiter has sports.

There's not a lot to say about sports on Jupiter, so bridging makes sense. How? Well, note the keywords: *sports* and *planet Jupiter*. You could transition to talking about sports in general, or planets in general. Let's try sports:

"You'd need to be extremely fit," you might begin, "to play any sport on Jupiter because of the intense gravitational pull. The good thing is that you'd only need to exercise for a few seconds each day—maybe just get out of bed—to stay in amazing shape, whereas on Earth, you need to work out much longer. I usually . . ." and now you bridge to your own exercise routine.

When the Question Is Too Personal, Decline

When President Bill Clinton was asked in 1994 whether he wore boxers or briefs, you expected him to decline.

(Or to *bridge*: "I think what you're really asking is who am I as a person, inside. Let me speak to that.")

Unfortunately, he answered.

The 17-year-old girl who asked Clinton, at an MTV town hall, said, "All the world's dying to know." But all the world wasn't; most of the world didn't even want to think about it.

In 2012, presidential candidate Mitt Romney was asked what he wore to bed. "As little as possible," he said. Most of the world didn't want to think about that either.

Why do leaders answer these questions? Well, to appear approachable, or likable, or real.

The message of Bill Clinton's presidency, wrote *Chicago Tribune* columnist Bob Greene: "The president is just a guy. There's no distance between the president and the people"[2]

But a leader needs distance. It's hard to imagine a U.S. president before Clinton talking about underwear. Now, these questions are routine.

I usually advise business leaders to welcome questions, to step into them, and to stay loose and relaxed.

But when the question is inappropriate, do the opposite. Put up your hands (as if stopping traffic), possibly smile (unless the question is too offensive), and say something like, "I don't think I'm going anywhere near that one." Then move on.

Or even simpler: "Thanks. Next question."

The nightmare interview question: "What's your biggest weakness?"

It's a test, how well do you handle yourself? You've got to answer, but without revealing too little or too much.

Some bad answers:

- *I'm wanted in three states for grand larceny.*

Too much. If you have to go this route, stick with *larceny*, delete *grand*. Grand sounds like a boast.

- *I have no weaknesses.*

Too little, too defensive.

- *I'm a perfectionist.*

Too cute.

- *I'm highly critical of other people's footwear.*

Too odd, though original.

The ideal answer is: job-related, already known, and fixable.

For example, if you've only worked for Fortune 500 companies, and you're applying for a nonprofit job, mention your lack of nonprofit experience—that's certainly a weakness.

But also mention: You're a fast learner, and you've done extensive volunteer work. Plus, you've had lots of experience in the airline industry, and none of those companies ever made a profit either.

CHAPTER 10

Presentation Tricks

"All the great speakers were bad speakers at first."
—RALPH WALDO EMERSON,
poet, essayist, lecturer

Open with Flair

No one in the audience spoke Japanese. But that didn't stop the speaker. His non-English opening lasted several minutes and stole the show.

The U.S. audience (senior leaders at a global company) looked spellbound. "I experienced," the person next to me said later, "what it feels like to work outside our U.S. headquarters."

True, the speaker also used slides, in English, to translate. For the audience, it was like reading subtitles in a foreign film. But many people avoid foreign films precisely because they dislike subtitles.

So what made this opening work? Well, it was different.

When you stand up and speak, your audience experiences you like a movie. Their first thought: is this movie interesting? And they may only give you 8 seconds to find out.

One Saturday night, my wife and I were at home, desperate to watch a movie. After scrolling through 1,000 bad choices, we rented *African Queen*, an old Humphrey Bogart film. Bogart won an Academy Award for his performance.

But that was 1951. Watch it today, the pace is deadly. Nothing happens for a very, very long time.

Are you a 1950s movie? You might be if you open your presentation by:

→ Putting up a slide with your talk's title, then reading it. Don't. Start with a dark screen, then flash the title a minute or two into your presentation.

→ Thanking everyone. Giving credit is good, but modern movies don't open that way. The credits come later.

→ Telling the audience that you'll be brief. Audiences appreciate brief, but is that really the best thing about your talk? Sounds less like a good movie, more like a bad commercial.

What to do instead?

10 Ways to Open Your Next Presentation

All these openings are before saying hello, good morning, or anything else. And each one would be followed by a compelling purpose statement. (Note: The 10 openings can overlap.)

1. **Question.** Questions are hard to resist, they engage our curiosity. Keep your opening question short and simple, but prepare it in advance.

   Example (from my workshop, *Your Point*): "Do you think attention spans are increasing or decreasing?"

   Decide whether your question is real (you expect an answer) or rhetorical (you don't), so you'll know whether to take a long or short pause.

2. **Quiz.** If you have a lot of learning points, try opening with a short, true-false quiz. Distribute the quiz, let participants complete it, then discuss.

   Example: If you were giving a talk on energy, your quiz might have 10–15 questions in total on nutrition, exercise, stress, etc.

Each question would relate to a key point and preview your presentation.

3. **"You're probably thinking" (or feeling or wondering).** The word "you" gets attention.

Suppose I'm sitting in your audience. There I am, thinking about me. That's human nature. But then you announce that you're also thinking about me. That makes me curious: "What are you thinking about what I'm thinking?"

Reading this, you're probably thinking, "How do I know what my audience is thinking? Half the time, I don't even know what I'm thinking."

But it's not that difficult, especially if you suspect your audience is not thrilled to be there. Name their objection right away. Then solve it with your purpose statement.

Example (from my workshop, *Bulletproof Feedback*): "You're probably thinking that feedback is dangerous. What if it backfires, what if the other person reacts emotionally, what if, later, his performance gets even worse?"

4. **"Imagine."** You can ask your audience to imagine something positive (e.g., imagine hiking along a mountain trail), or negative (imagine being pursued by mountain lions). "Imagine . . ." gets your audience visually absorbed.

Example (from my workshop, *10-Speed Thinking*): "Imagine that you and I are in a bicycle race. I've got a one-speed, black Schwinn bike—the one I grew up with—but you've got a 10-speed bike. You'll leave me in the dust."

When I use the above opening, it turns into an analogy: "10-Speed Thinking is like a 10-speed bike. You may never use all the speeds, but when you get stuck, shift gears."

5. **Analogy.** Like *imagine*, and like *story*, the visual is key.

Example (from my workshop, *Smart Questions*): "Asking smart questions is like cracking open a safe. You never know what you'll discover, but it's probably something valuable."

Notice that while "smart questions" is abstract, "cracking open a safe" is concrete and visual.

6. **Story.** A story, as we've discussed, is like a mini-presentation. And the first line of a story, like the first line of a presentation, should hook your audience.

Example (from my workshop, *Challenging Conversations*): "Midnight, and I'd just settled into my hotel room when the phone rang—I knew it wasn't going to be good."

7. **Demo/show.** Show beats tell (more on page 99, *Don't Just Tell—Show*).

Example (from my workshop, *Dynamic Speaking*): "I'm going to leave the room, and when I come back, I'll show you how NOT to do a presentation. See how many mistakes you can catch."

True, it would be faster to simply list the mistakes on a PowerPoint slide, but that's not nearly as effective as demonstrating them.

8. **Key word, number, or phrase.** Short beats long. You don't need a full sentence; if you throw out a word or number, it has mystery.

Example (from my workshop, *Accelerate Your Career*): "81,000 hours" (pause). "81,000 hours" (pause). "That's how much time, roughly, you'll work in your life. And in the wrong job, every day will feel that long."

9. **Quote.** If you use a quote, make sure to attribute it.

Example (from my workshop, *When Leaders Speak*): "Every time you speak, you are auditioning for leadership."

I love this quote from former presidential speechwriter James Humes. (Look for it later in the book.)

10. **Unusual fact.** Tell your audience something they don't know.

Example (from my keynote, *Resilience@Work*): "How many thoughts a day do you have?" (Pause, then give answer): "60,000."

Another combo here: The question sets up the unusual fact.

60,000 thoughts? That's why your audience is so distracted, and why you need to hook them right away.

Surprise Them with Something Unusual

Everybody is obsessed with Alexander Hamilton these days, thanks to the hit Broadway musical.

Do you remember how Hamilton died?

a. Snake bite
b. Killed by Aaron Burr
c. Killed by Raymond Burr

You already know the answer is "b"—although as someone who's concerned about snakes, I think "a" is a reasonable guess.

(As for "c," Raymond Burr was a suspected murderer, but only in the Hitchcock film *Rear Window*. He was best known for playing the TV character Perry Mason.)

Do you know how any of the other U.S. Founding Fathers died? I don't. But we remember Hamilton's death because it was unusual (*variety*).

Ever feel restless at a meeting because there's nothing new or surprising? "My clients," a manager told me, "barely pay attention at our meetings. They're riveted to their phones."

"What's the purpose of these meetings?" I asked.

"To review the deck," the manager said. (You may remember from chapter 2 that "reviewing the deck" is not a purpose; it's an agenda item.)

"What do you mean by *review*?" I asked.

"Well, we send out all the important information in advance," he said. "Then we go over it in detail at the meeting."

From the clients' perspective (*be the audience*), there's no real benefit. And the information is stale. Solution? Either repurpose the meeting or cancel it.

Don't Surprise Them—Be Dull

Does it ever pay to be deliberately dull?

Yes! Although I shudder to say so because usually the answer is NO. Too many presentations lack zest.

You've been there, in the audience, pretending to listen, straining to stay awake, counting the minutes left in the meeting or the number of slides left in the deck.

And yet, occasionally, dull works; exciting doesn't.

After Janet Yellen became chairwoman of the Federal Reserve, she appeared before Congress to present the Fed's semi-annual Monetary Policy Report.

What she said was entirely predictable. Predictable was the point.

"I am a sensible central banker," she said, responding to the question, "Are you a sensible central banker?"

What kind of question, by the way, is that? Well, for one thing, it's closed, with either a yes or no answer. "No" would be intriguing:

"No, Congressman, I'm not a sensible banker. I'm not even, really, a banker." Then, *laugh hysterically.* *"I'm a wild and crazy person, pretending to be a banker."* More laughing. *"Just ask my colleagues, they'll tell you—I'm completely insane. And I control the money supply. All of it, every last penny!"*

If you're running the Fed—an organization created in response to financial PANIC—your job is to look and sound sensible. And Ms. Yellen, with her deep knowledge and experience, certainly did.

She thanked lawmakers twice that day for calling her *unexciting*.

But here's what was unexpected: she offered to stay the entire day.

The head of the congressional committee thanked her for the offer. "Madam Chair," he said, "you're in luck. We're not staying all day."

But they stayed almost six hours. That's a long time for Q & A. And her endurance sent an important message too.[1]

Ms. Yellen's audience that day was not regular people like you and me. It was the global financial markets, running trillions of dollars, euros, yen, and yuan—an audience desperately hoping for dull (*be the audience*).

Don't Just Tell—Show

Let's say your presentation is about the Chinese stock market. It's been falling, you explain. Meanwhile, your audience is falling asleep.

Can you liven things up? Consider three options:

1. **PowerPoint:** There's always PowerPoint. You could, I suppose, illustrate the stock market drop with a bar graph or a line graph displaying the downward trend.

   Perfectly reasonable, which is why it won't wake anyone up. (We'll discuss some PowerPoint tricks later.)

2. **Whiteboard:** Silently, walk over to a whiteboard or flip chart and, remaining silent, draw a descending arrow. Then step away, point to the arrow, and say, "That's the Chinese stock market."

   The trick here is to stay silent for three to five seconds. That's hard for many presenters; that's why it works.

3. **Prop:** Take a plastic cup, hold it in front of you, and say, "Here's the Chinese stock market." Then drop the cup. Wait for the cup to hit the floor and make a sound. Then talk. (Or, at that point, show a slide with some details.)

These options range from very common (PowerPoint) to less common (props). I recommend less common. Remember: *be slightly different.*

Slightly different captures attention. Plus, you'll look skilled and confident.

Notice, though, that all three options involve *showing*. You may remember, when you were a little kid in school, an activity called "show and tell." The idea was to not just tell the class something, but also to show something.

So if you were talking about the beach, you could bring in a pail filled with sand and pass it around. The other kids could see the sand, or touch it, or pour it over someone's head.

Show beats tell. Show engages our senses and engages us. Show adds color to the usual biz presentation.

So consider some showmanship at your next presentation. Try using a prop once in a while. And don't worry about whether your prop matches the thing you're talking about.

If an empty cup can be the Chinese stock market, then anything can be anything. And, at your next presentation, you can be anything too.

p.s. Bad props: Avoid pouring sand on someone's head. That exceeds slightly different.

Also, the minute everyone starts using a certain technique, for example, dropping plastic cups, stop using that technique. It's no longer slightly different.

Props: Another Example

It's 6 a.m. and Mika looks exasperated.

She co-hosts *Morning Joe*, a talk show on MSNBC. This morning, Joe, the other co-host, plus assorted guests, are busy eating junk cereal.

I'm on an elliptical machine in my basement, working out and watching all this in a desperate attempt to forget I'm working out.

Usually, Mika and Joe spar about politics. But today they're arguing about Frosted Flakes, Lucky Charms, and Cap'n Crunch.

Mika finally takes all the cereal boxes and dumps them in the trash, at which point Joe says something like, "Don't think I won't take the cereal out of there and eat it."

Why is this so entertaining? I wonder.

Here's one reason: props. Those cereal boxes grab us.

When you say junk food is good (or bad), that's *telling*. When you eat Frosted Flakes (or dump them), that's *showing*.

Showing is visual. Like watching TV, it steals your attention. You temporarily forget that it's 6 a.m., that you're on an elliptical, and that you'd rather be sleeping—or eating vast quantities of Froot Loops.

The problem with most business info, which we've discussed before (with analogies and stories) is that it's abstract and hard to see. It's even harder to eat or digest.

Props solve that problem.

Imagine you're giving a presentation about a predicament that confronts almost every organization: different groups/departments don't understand each other.

I once coached an executive for a similar presentation. The exec faced his audience and—without saying a word—took a few water bottles and placed each one on a different table in the room.

No one knew what he was up to; everyone paid attention.

Then he said, "This is the way we work—in silos." He talked about that for a while: the cost of silos, a few solutions.

(As mentioned, with props, you don't need to be literal. A water bottle, for example, can be anything, even an abstract idea like working in silos.)

At the end, he retrieved the bottles and poured all the water into one pitcher. "Break down the barriers," he said . . .

Break down the barriers that block attention. Try props.

Got Slides? Treat Each One as a Mini-Presentation

Here's the best approach:

1. **Overview the slide.** Don't jump right into the details; give an overview first. Say something like, "What we're looking at here," or "What this slide is about . . ."

   Sure, you've been thinking about your slides for a while, but your audience is just seeing them for the first time. Remember the curse of knowledge (page 57)? "Don't assume we know more than we do.

   Be the audience.

2. **Give appropriate detail** (*focus*). What does your audience really need to know? It's probably less than you want to say.

3. **Give the key point.** Just like the presentation itself, each slide should have a single most important thing. A good phrase: "The most important thing about this slide is . . ."

4. **Transition to the next slide.** If you're not going to use another slide for a while, darken the screen.

My favorite PowerPoint move: press the "B" button on your laptop to make the screen black. Then press "B" again when you want it back on.

If you do.

How many slides should you use?

I usually say 10, only because it's a finite number and it's less than 1,000.

A better answer: it depends.

It depends, for example, on whether your audience can see you. If so, use fewer slides—or none.

But if you're leading a virtual meeting, and you're invisible to the audience, change your slides every minute or so to keep things moving.

And to give them something to *see*.

More on Slides: Use Three Ways to Capture Attention

Suppose you're preparing a presentation about the stock market called "How to Stay Up When the Market Goes Down."

Your main slide is about corrections (a market plunge of 10% or more) and looks like this:

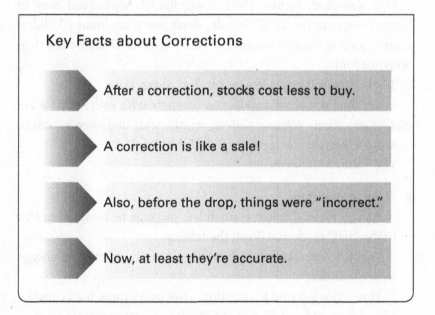

Ok, let's improve it.

1. Better titles.

A title, like any good headline, should attract attention. "Key Facts about Corrections" is bland. Strengthen your title with one of these options:

- a. A question, such as, "What Are Smart Investors Doing Now?" or "Is 3 a.m. a Good Time to Review Your Portfolio?" or "What's the Best Time of Day to Panic?"
- b. A provocative statement, for example, " 4 Good Things about Losing All Your Money."
- c. A surprising fact, for example, "Avg. Recovery Time from a Crash: 3.3 Years."[2]

2. Less text.

The fewer words, the better. In the sample slide, I've used full sentences, but that only works if you're going to email the deck, not present it.

Pare down to keywords.

Guy Kawasaki, former chief evangelist of Apple (and now of Canva) suggests the *10-20-30 rule*: don't use more than 10 slides, don't talk more than 20 minutes, and, my favorite, don't use *less* than 30-point font.

30-point font is large: less words, less distraction.

Every time you show a slide, you compete with your slide for audience attention. When a slide is wordy, your audience wonders, "Should I listen to the speaker or read the slide?"

Their solution: daydream.

3. More interaction.

As you move through your slides, you may be tempted to stay in the "tell" mode and do all the talking.

Don't. It kills attention. Instead, get your audience to engage with the slides.

How? You guessed it, questions. Not every time, but occasionally, show a slide, and—instead of talking—ask something.

For example, if I had a summary slide about these three techniques, I'd show a picture of a comatose audience. No words, except maybe a title: "They're Asleep, But It's Your Nightmare"

Then I'd say, "We talked about three ways to wake 'em up: titles, text, and interaction." Then I'd ask, "If you could only use one thing, which would you use?"

(I suggest all three.)

Talk About Food

Recently, the World Health Organization (WHO) said some unpleasant things about meat. Namely, that it's sort of carcinogenic.

This story grabbed the media's attention, and maybe yours too. But why? Why do certain messages break through the clutter—and how can you do that?

Here's one clue: food. The mere mention of food hooks people. Your next presentation probably isn't about food. But don't let that stop you from a quick reference now and then.

I remember listening to a CEO deliver an all-company voice mail. "I'm in the kitchen with my kids," he began, "making strawberry jam." He then went on to talk about the company.

The next day, I didn't remember a single thing he'd said, except for the jam. I don't even like jam.

That CEO could have been cooking anything—blueberry pancakes, fried eggs, some crispy, carcinogenic bacon. Food gets attention.

What the President Ate for Lunch

Consider a New York Times article on a lunch the U.S. President hosted for congressional leaders. The story wasn't about the food, but that was the most interesting detail.

"Herb-crusted sea-bass and pumpkin tarts," reported the Times.[3]

And each guest left with a six-pack of Honey Ale beer, brewed right at the White House.

Otherwise, not much happened regarding gridlock.

There's a "bitterness," said Garrett Oliver, and "it's not without complexity."

Mr. Oliver wasn't commenting on the politics, but on the White House beer. He's a brewmaster.[4]

To engage your audience, you may need to be a bit of a brewmaster too. Find ways to add color.

Talk More about Food

Why does the mere mention of food beat most business info? Well, for one thing, we like thinking about food, and there's a lot to consider:

- → What did I just eat?
- → What else could I eat—and when?
- → How much food is reasonable for one person to actually consume in a day?
- → Why is there never anything good in the refrigerator?
- → Is it bad to skip breakfast?
- → Why is everyone eating so much kale?
- → Can anyone recommend a good diet?

But there's something else about food: it's concrete and easy to visualize.

The other day, while coaching an executive on a presentation, I kept thinking about Froot Loops, a breakfast cereal mentioned earlier. (More Froot Loops in a second.)

The presentation was about the Quality Maturity Model. That's an important topic, but notice how abstract each word is (*quality . . . maturity . . . model*). You can't really picture the Quality Maturity Model. And you certainly can't eat it.

We flagged the problem with abstraction earlier (analogies and stories). Let's illustrate the difference between abstract vs. concrete with a concrete example—about food.

"This morning," I might say, "I ate:

➡ "Foodstuff." Totally abstract—this could be any substance, according to my dictionary, with food value. Sounds unpleasant.
➡ "A bowl of cereal." Beats foodstuff, but still very generic.
➡ "An entire carton of, you guessed it, Froot Loops."
➡ "Two four-minute eggs, a rasher of broiled bacon, orange juice, and milk."

Froot Loops and four-minute eggs are easy to visualize, so they're more likely to grab your audience's attention and be remembered.

About those four-minute eggs and bacon: not only can you see it, you can smell it, taste it, and hear it (sizzling bacon). It's also, according to a book, what John F. Kennedy ate for breakfast every day.[5]

That's the only thing I remember from the book. Although if JFK had been consuming vast quantities of Froot Loops, I might have recalled that too.

Food engages your senses in a way that ordinary business info doesn't. Still not convinced? Then Google the following:

➡ The Peanut Butter Manifesto: A famous Yahoo memo, which compared their unfocused pursuit of every opportunity to spreading peanut butter too thinly.
➡ The Sandwich Technique: A feedback method—it doesn't work, by the way—where you sandwich a critical message (the meat) between blander comments (the bread).
➡ The Swiss Cheese Method: A time management trick for getting started on a difficult task. Just spend a few minutes on your project, poke a few holes.[6]

Poke a few holes in your opaque abstractions. Illustrate your message with word-pictures, whether food or otherwise.

p.s. I don't actually eat Froot Loops. But I admire the holes.

Own the Room

Here are seven ways to do that:

1. **Avoid the podium.** Let's say you're the fifth presenter at a meeting, and the first four stand behind the podium. As you step on stage, that podium will have a strong gravitational pull.

   Resist.

   Your audience wants to see you; the more they see, the better. Get large.

2. **Move.** I recently watched a senior executive speak for 20 minutes without moving an inch.

   He looked frozen, as if the room were filled with wild animals, about to attack. That's the "Oh, no, I'm talking to an audience of grizzly bears!" look.

   That's not a good look.

   So move, and when you do, be decisive. Is it time to begin? Then walk to the front of the room and begin. Don't hesitate.

3. **When you get a question, step forward,** toward the audience.

   One step forward is all it takes. That beats stepping back (which looks like a retreat) or running around the room in circles (which looks amusing, but strange).

4. **Keep your hands in front of your body,** out of your pockets, and away from your hair and face.

5. **Gesture.** Gestures come in three sizes—small, medium, and large. Vary yours.

   If you were seated at a table, a small gesture would be pointing toward the water pitcher. Medium would be reaching to get it. Large would be knocking it over with enough force to send it flying across the room.

   Not to boast, but I'm extremely skilled at the latter.

6. **Look at individuals.** Check in: "How are you doing over there?" your eyes say.

If you think of your audience as a "they," you'll be out-numbered. Instead, see individuals. There is no "they."

7. **Speak louder.** Speak as though the room were twice as large and you wanted to be heard—all the way in the back. Speak as though you had a voice of thunder.

Speak as though your message mattered.

Break a Rule

When the current host of *Meet the Press*, the oldest TV show in the U.S., first took the job, he had an unusual on-air habit. We'll get to that shortly.

I wasn't surprised when the former host was replaced. He seemed depressed, as if the weight of the world had finally ground him down and he'd lost any shred of hope.

"The news this week," his expression seemed to say, "is just dismal."

The current host looks upbeat and energetic. But during his first few months, he'd sometimes deliver a brief commentary, standing up (that part is good—if you can stand, do it), while holding a rolled up paper.

Why the paper?

I figured he'd eventually unroll it and reveal something important or unexpected. "42," he might say (that's the meaning of life, according to *The Hitchhiker's Guide to the Galaxy*).[7]

But no, the paper always stayed rolled up.

"Lose the paper," others must have advised. "It serves no purpose, it's distracting."

"But the paper makes me happy," the host might say.

And it's true, when you're under pressure, holding onto something—a piece of paper, a large pointer, a small puppy—offers comfort.

But that's speaker-focused, not audience-focused.

Why not at least vary the prop? One week, you hold the paper; next week, a random shoe from one of your colleagues.

You could argue the paper reveals a lack of confidence. Maybe. But maybe someone suggested it to eliminate a worse habit. Or maybe this host is so confident that he simply doesn't care.

The truth is, over time, I've grown accustomed to the rolled up paper. Recently, I haven't seen him hold it. I sort of miss it.

That's the thing about a small human imperfection: it's authentic. And it's different.

So learn the rules of good form, and master them. Then, every so often, break a few. Because you also need to honor the variety that's you.

PART III

Capture Attention with PRESENCE

"Every time you speak, you are auditioning for leadership."

—JAMES HUMES
(speechwriter for four U.S. presidents)

You listen to certain people at work, but not to others, and sometimes it's just because of their presence. But what exactly is that?

Presence, or executive presence (used here interchangeably), sounds like an all-or-nothing mysterious thing—as if you either have it, or don't.

Let's demystify it.

What others know about you is based on their observations of your behavior, and then their inferences or guesses about what that behavior means.

Presence is really just an inference, made by others based on how you act.

Since actions are the key, we'll start with an important psychological principle: *Act as if.* You can act confident, for example, without feeling confident (chapter 11). Then, we'll identify 10 actions that contribute to *presence* (chapter 12).

The 10 actions fall into three categories: Image (chapter 13) includes everything from your nonverbal behavior to your LinkedIn profile.

Drive (chapter 14) is about getting results. For example, do you follow through on your commitments, even simple ones?

Temperament (chapter 15) shows up in numerous ways, such as how you react to others' ideas, and how you behave under stress.

There's good news here: you can increase your presence—and your odds of getting heard—with action.

CHAPTER 11

Act As If

"If you want a quality, act as if you already had it."

—WILLIAM JAMES, psychologist

*"I said, 'I don't think I can give you that kind of emotion.'
And he [Hitchcock] sat there and said, 'Ingrid, fake it!' Well,
that was the best advice I've had in my whole life."*

—INGRID BERGMAN, actress

What's the opposite of executive presence?

Executive absence. Here's what absence sounds like if, for example, you're giving a presentation. You begin with excuses:

"I'm not very good at this," you might say. "And I didn't receive the PowerPoint slides until a few minutes ago, and right after that, the entire left side of my body went completely numb."

The message: "Audience, don't expect too much. In fact, let's not focus on you at all. Let's worry about me."

Imagine if other professionals did this:

Pilot to passengers: "Gosh, this is the first time I've ever flown such a big plane. Our flight today may be a little jumpy. God knows, I am."

Doctor to patient: "Cover your mouth, and stop coughing so much. I'm just getting over a horrible stomach virus. I really feel gross—much worse than this stupid thing you've got."

U.S. President to country: "I've never given a State of the Union address before, and my schedule has been crazy busy, no rest at all, not even for a second. This is, by far, the worst job I've ever had. So please don't ask, 'How are things going in the USA?' I really have no idea."

What do doctors, pilots, and presidents have in common? Acting.

"There have been times in this office," Ronald Reagan said, "when I've wondered how you could do the job if you hadn't been an actor."[1]

But we're not talking about professional acting. We're talking about "acting as if," a powerful idea first promoted by William James (often called "the father of American psychology"), then later popularized as "fake it till you make it."

Years ago, a men's fashion magazine took some homeless men and gave them a complete makeover. Dressed up, the men looked like executives.

That's "acting as if," and that's roughly the same process you and I go through every morning when we struggle out of bed.

We need to suit up.

President Reagan's Best Joke

The remarkable thing was not the joke, but Reagan's timing.

The 69th day of his presidency, he'd been shot—the bullet was an inch from his heart—and he was telling his wife about the assassination attempt.

"Honey, I forgot to duck," he said, a line first used by boxer Jack Dempsey after losing a fight.

If someone shot me, I'm not sure I'd respond by joking around.

Sometimes I complain if I have a head cold or if my back is a little stiff, so I can't see being overly cheerful if there were a bullet lodged near my heart.

Also there's the trauma. Someone shot me! With a gun! At the very least, my feelings would be hurt.

> But not Reagan. He refused to look or act distressed—that's what his humor said. "I hope you're all Republicans," he joked with the surgeons.
>
> Ok, so he wasn't hysterically funny. But the surgeons must have been impressed by his presence.
>
> So was the country—Reagan's approval rating soared to 73%.

Confidence: Avoid These Three Mistakes

Mistake #1: Assuming you know what's going on inside others.

Suppose at the next leadership offsite, your CEO stands up and then, in a commanding voice, sings out the quarterly financials.

You're impressed. And yet, you know nothing about the CEO's inner experience. He could be extremely confident, or extremely nervous, or extremely insane.

Mistake #2: Assuming others know what's going on inside you.

Let's say you're at a meeting, feeling stressed. But if your heart is pounding, others can't hear it. And if you've got butterflies in your belly, others can't see them.

Often, the only reason others know you're nervous is because you feel compelled to tell everyone.

Don't.

Mistake #3: Assuming you should feel as confident inside as others appear outside.

"Stop comparing your insides to others' outsides."

That's my favorite line (paraphrased) from a novel about a U.S. President whose physician vanishes.[2] Then the President has a psychotic episode, which, to me, just seemed like a predictable reaction to bad health care.

When I work with business leaders, they're often surprised to discover a basic truth: *You can act confident without feeling confident.*

And if you act confident enough times, eventually the feeling will show up.

Don't wait.

CHAPTER 12

Ten Actions to Increase Your Presence: Assess Yourself

"I've missed more than 9,000 shots in my career. I've lost almost 300 games. 26 times, I've been trusted to take the game winning shot and missed. I've failed over and over and over again in my life. And that is why I succeed."

—MICHAEL JORDAN, basketball star

Let's take this vague notion of *presence* and make it more specific and actionable.

Review the 10 items that follow, which we'll group into three themes:

1. Your image
2. Your drive
3. Your temperament

What are you doing well? Find two to three items. What could you do better? Find two to three items. How do your colleagues see you? Ask them.

Or, if you prefer, score each item on a 1–10 scale (1 low; 5 average; 10 high). You can give the same score to different items, but avoid giving everything a 5.

It's important with lists like this to avoid being overly self-critical. No one is great at everything. What are your strengths? Build on them.

Note: These 10 items are not a definition of leadership (leaders need presence, so all the items apply, but so do other items not on this list). And it's certainly not the last word. Executive presence varies across organizations, cultures, and countries.

This list is grounded in my consulting work, over 25 years, with executives and managers at leading companies and, although not scientific, it's been tested with more than a thousand workshop participants.

Here's what we're trying to figure out: What is it about you and your *presence* that makes others listen, or not listen? These 10 items will give you some actionable ideas.

Your image:

1. **Nonverbals:** Projects confidence with voice and body language. (Voice: volume, speed, pitch, pauses, clarity. Body language: facial expression, eye contact, posture, movement, gestures.)

2. **Optics:** Attends to physical appearance, office appearance, social media appearance, as well as language and behavior in formal and informal settings to set high standards.

Your drive:

3. **Focus:** Stays focused at meetings and at work on what's most important. Is fully present. Gives the right amount of detail to the right audiences.

4. **Energy:** Projects physical, emotional, and mental energy (physical means you're animated; emotional, you care; mental, you're alert). Sustains energy over time.

5. **Initiative:** Offers ideas and suggestions to continuously improve and innovate. Experiments with new approaches, takes calculated risks. Is proactive.

6. **Commitment:** Makes and keeps commitments. Takes responsibility for getting things done. Stays true to one's values. Persists, persists, persists.

Your temperament:

7. **Humility:** Admits and learns from mistakes. Seeks and values others' ideas and involvement. Listens with respect. Shares credit.

8. **Command:** Takes the lead. Speaks up. Asserts oneself skillfully, without either aggression or undue concern for being liked or agreed with.

9. **Optimism:** Takes a positive approach to problems and tasks. Imagines and communicates a positive, credible future state.

10. **Composure:** Demonstrates calm under pressure. Handles stressful situations well. Thinks on one's feet, improvises. Uses humor appropriately.

These 10 items, of course, interact. For example, your optimism influences your energy. (Ever feel hopeless? That's generally not a high-energy state.)

Back to the three themes. They're based on three questions your audience is trying to assess (*be the audience*).

Three Themes	Based on Three Questions
1. Image	1. Do you look and sound the part?
2. Drive	2. Do you get results?
3. Temperament	3. Do you have the right disposition?

In the following chapters, we'll look at some examples, good and bad, of these 10 items. Notice how fast they work. Often, in seconds.

CHAPTER 13

Image: Communicate that You Look and Sound the Part

"Acting is not about being someone different. It's finding the similarity in what is apparently different, then finding myself in there."

—MERYL STREEP, actress

Two items from chapter 12 go here:

➡ **Nonverbals:** Projects confidence with voice and body language (Voice: volume, speed, pitch, pauses, clarity. Body language: facial expression, eye contact, posture, movement, gestures.)

➡ **Optics:** Attends to physical appearance, office appearance, social media appearance, as well as language and behavior in formal and informal settings to set high standards.

Clients sometimes ask which of the 10 presence actions is most important. Depends on your audience. How do other execs in your organization act? What do they value?

But without knowing your organization, I'd pick nonverbals. Your voice and body language shape others' perceptions, instantly (remember Harriet, from page xvii?)

Optics is closely related. What do your clothing and grooming communicate? How about your LinkedIn profile? How do you handle time—are you prompt or always late? How do you behave at work parties?

Presence Action #1: Nonverbals

Watch Your Eye Contact

Bad eye contact almost killed me. I was in a NYC subway. A big muscular guy, seated opposite me, had a baseball bat that he kept tapping into his left palm.

He looked angry, and he was staring at me as if to say, "Obviously, it's all your fault."

If this guy were giving a presentation, let's say on "How to Resolve 10 Everyday Problems with a Baseball Bat," he'd be making a classic mistake: looking at just one person in the audience (me!) at the expense of everyone else.

Of course, no one else in the subway was looking at anyone. They certainly weren't looking at this guy.

What is good eye contact anyway? A lot of people have taken the wrong subway or read the wrong book.

Good eye contact is *not* continuous. I've interviewed job candidates who thought it was continuous—they never take their eyes off you. Please don't do that. It's scary.

In general, three to five seconds is about right; the person listening usually looks longer than the one speaking. But it really depends on whom you're looking at, and where you are.

Maybe you're in an elevator. Or maybe you're out hiking and, suddenly, you're facing a grizzly bear. What if you're in an elevator with a grizzly bear? I'd say three to five seconds is a tad long, unless you and the bear ride up together every day.

And three to five seconds may be too long if you're in a non-Western culture or talking with a really shy person.

The subway guy didn't look shy, so after a while I looked him in the eye to let him know, in no uncertain terms, "Buddy, your three to five seconds are up."

Then I looked away, to let him know, "I'm certainly willing to consider an extension."

He got off at the next stop. I'm sure it was the way I handled it . . .

Avoid these mistakes:

➡ Looking too long.

➡ Not long enough. (Tip: Look until you see the color of the person's eyes.)

➡ In a group, only looking at the people you like, or who are most influential, or who may or may not have baseball bats.

Listen to How You Sound

Can a monotone voice land you in jail?

After the jury in a big insider trading case delivered a "Guilty on all counts" verdict, one of the jurors told *The Wall Street Journal* her impressions of the defense attorney:

His voice was "monotone." He seemed "tired."[1]

Of course, the evidence didn't help either. But consider:

1. If you're an executive pitching a business plan, what determines the outcome?
2. If you're a surgeon, what determines if you get sued?

Often, it's your voice.

MIT professor Alex Pentland demonstrated that you can predict winning business pitches without paying any attention to the content.

Instead, he focused on critical nonverbal behaviors, like vocal variety.[2]

Similarly, you can predict which surgeons will get sued just by listening to their tone of voice for 40 seconds, even if you can't understand a word they're saying.

The worst tone for surgeons? Dominant. That's according to psychologist Nalini Ambady.[3]

How's your voice?

The lawyer in the insider trading case assumed his voice was fine. It wasn't.

The easiest way to check how you sound is voice mail. Record a new outgoing message, then critique it. If you phone me, you'll hear something like this, "Hi, this is Paul Hellman, the week of May 30th . . ."

I change my message weekly. It's good practice. And it's good to reassure everyone that you were definitely alive on the 29th.

To sound alive is no small thing.

Leaving a voicemail?

Consider your message a mini-presentation: you've got seconds to make a good impression.

Let's apply seven classic presentation skills to your voice message:

1. Adapt to your audience. Even if you're calling someone you've never met, you still get to hear her outgoing message before leaving yours. Listen carefully. Then adapt.

If she speaks fast, then you speak fast. If her message is concise, then you be concise.

If her message mentions something significant—"Hi it's Jacqueline. I'm in the Arctic today being pursued by wolverines"—then respond accordingly: "Oh, that sounds just like my office."

2. Structure your message. Jot down some keywords, or prepare a loose script. Just don't sound scripted.

Any important message—even a 30-second voice mail— should have an opening, middle, and close. Opening: who are you and why are you calling; middle: critical details, if any; close: next steps.

There's a message on my phone from someone named Fred. Fred wants to talk, but doesn't say why. This week Fred called again. "I'm calling to follow up on my message from last week."

I haven't called Fred back yet. I feel guilty about Fred.

3. Give the right amount of detail. Usually that means less.

4. Watch your nonverbals. Even if no one can see you, body language still matters. Stand up (you'll project better), move

around (you'll sound more dynamic), and smile (you'll sound more friendly).

Suppose you're working at home—can the person on the other end of the phone tell if you're still in pajamas? Some experts say yes! I don't think so, but I avoid calling anyone in my pajamas. I don't even own pajamas.

Then there's your outgoing message. That's a mini-presentation too.

5. Be upbeat. After all, it's an "outgoing" message. True, you don't want to sound too cheerful, but many people sound downright glum.

One executive I called last week had an outgoing message that ended with "make it a GREAT day." Normally I don't go in for that sort of thing, but he sounded really genuine and I appreciated his spirit.

On the other hand, I wasn't exactly sure how to make it a GREAT day; that made me feel worse.

6. Keep it fresh. For example, as discussed earlier, mention the date: "Hi this is Tyler on Thursday, May 7." This works especially well if it really is May 7—and you really are Tyler.

7. Set realistic expectations. Some people promise to call you back within 30 minutes. Impressive! But if you make a promise like that, you've got to follow through.

Even if it means calling Fred.

Make Your Words and Non-words Match— Unless They Shouldn't

In poker, they call it a "tell."

One night after dinner, my daughter, then five, wanted ice cream.

"Had any sweets today, honey?" I asked.

"No." Then she smiled involuntarily, as if to say, "I've been eating vast quantities of sugar all day and night, you idiot."

She quickly realized her mistake. "Wait Daddy," she said. "Ask me again."

Nonverbal signals. We watch them because they often "tell" the truth, unless you're dealing with a sharp poker player, a trained actor, or a very experienced sociopath.

When the words and the body language don't match, that's a mixed message, and we trust the body language. Some mixed messages are ok, others not. Here are three examples:

1. **Bad mixed message:** A CEO I know never smiles. That makes his feedback confusing.

   Suppose he says you're doing a "good job." The words sound fine, but his flat voice and non-smile signal trouble. "Good job" sounds like "not good enough."

   "Something bad is about to happen to you," the CEO's body language suggests, "but given your performance, it's probably not bad enough."

2. **Neutral mixed message:** You're walking around the office, and you spot a colleague. "How are you?" you ask.

   Then, before he can say, "I've got a bad case of swine flu," you sprint past him in a mad dash down the hall, as if to say, "I need to get away from you, right now!"

   Well, that's definitely a mixed message. But everyone does it.

3. **Good mixed message:** Suppose you need to say "no."

   "Bob, I'd love to help you," you might say in a pleasant voice, "organize the team-building retreat for our European office. And you're right, running with the bulls is something we've never done before, and it's good to know there's only a slight risk of getting gored or trampled to death. But I'm really tied up right now."

   Your message is clear: You won't be able to get to Bob's project today, tomorrow, or, really, ever. But you can send that message in a friendly way.

Generally, for a good-news message (*You're hired!*), or a bad-news message (*You're fired!*), it's best if your words and nonverbals match.

But occasionally, it pays to send a mixed message. When your words need to be strong and assertive, but you also need to maintain the relationship, soften your body language.

What to Say When You're Not Talking

If you were an actor playing a love scene, it might be helpful, as you look at your romantic partner, to think, *You have lovely eyes.* You wouldn't say it, you'd just think it.

Less helpful: *Did you eat a pastrami sandwich for breakfast?*

Your thoughts can increase (or decrease) your ability to look and sound the part. Why not create a few extra-strength ones?

A mantra is a word or phrase you tell yourself, silently, to evoke a desired quality such as confidence, or energy, or calm. Although mantras sound exotic, they're not. You and I think certain thoughts, again and again, every day. These repetitive thoughts are mantras, but some are better than others.

A few bad mantras:

• "My boss is an idiot."

Do you often think this? Bingo—you've got a mantra!

Unfortunately, the "idiot" mantra will eventually leak into your nonverbal behavior and become obvious to others, including your boss, so you may want to change it.

• "I'm tired."

When the alarm goes off in the morning, we often think, *tired.* Then we attempt to calculate X, where X = how much sleep we got. The one thing we know about X: it wasn't enough.

Ever notice that telling yourself how tired you feel doesn't really help?

"I'm completely exhausted," you think. "But wait, now that I've said that, suddenly my energy has skyrocketed!" Not likely.

Since you're already using mantras, why not try one or two positive ones? Suppose, for example, you're preparing for a job interview, a performance appraisal, or a bad dental experience. Desired quality: confidence. To trigger the quality, try a phrase like *strong and confident* for a minute or so.

You can reinforce this with a picture, for example, strong and confident like a bull (picture a bull), or with a memory (recall an experience when you felt strong and confident).

Another variation: sync the words with your breath, as meditation teacher Thich Nhat Hanh advises; for example, *breathing in, strong; breathing out, confident.*

Keep it short and simple, but experiment with different words. Which ones evoke a positive feeling?

Sometimes, before you can influence others, you need to inspire yourself.

Presence Action #2: Optics

Watch Your Clothing—On or Off

Do you pay too little, or too much, attention to optics?

Example #1: Too little attention.

An accountant, at a large public accounting firm, met with a key client for three hours and wore his overcoat the whole time.

The client was offended and later complained. He felt the accountant couldn't wait to bolt out the door.

Why didn't the accountant take off his coat? One can speculate:

➡ He was cold.
➡ He was worried that someone would steal the coat.
➡ He had stolen the coat.
➡ It wasn't really a coat. It just looked like a coat.

Example # 2: Too much attention.

A related situation with coats involved Ronald Reagan when he first met Gorbachev. Reagan wanted to wear a coat because it was a cold November day in Geneva, and he was going outside to greet Gorbachev's motorcade.

But an advisor persuaded Reagan, after a long argument, to remove it because, if Gorbachev showed up coatless and Reagan was bundled up, Reagan would look old and frail by comparison.

Gorbachev arrived wearing a coat, scarf, and hat. He probably thought Reagan looked strange.[4]

p.s. Back to the accountant: He'd spilled coffee on his shirt before the meeting and wore the coat to hide the stain.

p.p.s. I just made that up. But clearly the client wondered about the accountant, and his coat, for a while.

Social Media? Avoid These LinkedIn Mistakes

Let's talk about LinkedIn, the most career-relevant media. An important moment is when you invite others to link. Four common mistakes:

1. Never inviting anyone.
Hmm, this one's tempting. No one likes rejection, it forces you to relive high school.

I remember having a high school crush on Linda S. One night, I finally called for a date.

"Who exactly are you?" Linda S. asked.

"I sit on the opposite side of the room in English," I said. That didn't really explain who I was. It didn't even explain, really, where I was.

More about Linda S. in a moment.

Meanwhile, some good news: high school's over. When you invite people to LinkedIn, some will accept, others won't. Nothing terrible will befall you.

2. Bad timing.

When I called Linda S. for a date, my timing was flawed, but only in the sense that it was already Saturday night.

"Yes," Linda S. said, "I'd love to go out, and I think my date's at the door right now."

Timing matters. Are your LinkedIn invitations too late or too early?

"Don't invite within two hours of meeting," says Rod Hughes, Vice President, Kimball Communications. "I typically wait till the next day," he says. "Anything sooner seems stalker-esque."

3. Inviting everyone.

Suppose you wake up one morning determined to network with a European chancellor.

"How do you know Angela Merkel?" LinkedIn will ask, as if already suspicious.

"Colleague," you say. But if she gets your invitation (which of course she won't) and tells LinkedIn she's never heard of you, LinkedIn won't like that. You'll be penalized.

"You need a policy," says Thom Singer, author of several networking books. "My policy," he says, "is the Coffee, Meal, or Beer Rule, which means not accepting links unless I've had a real conversation."

4. Bad invitation.

I remember one that made me nervous: "Add me," the invitation began. "I'm adding you to my LinkedIn network. Please accept." Sounded less like an invitation, more like an order.

At LinkedIn, the default invite is, "I'd like to add you to my professional network." But sending the default is robotic.

Make your invitations personal. Here are two examples, sent to CEOs by Eric Fischgrund, Founder of FischTank Marketing and PR:

➡ "Met your staff at the trade show—looking forward to learning more."
➡ "Congrats on the earnings announcement! Please keep us in mind for marketing/PR initiatives moving forward."

"My cardinal rule," says Fischgrund: "never use the default."
Good rule (*variety*).

CHAPTER 14

Drive: Communicate that You Get Results

"Dear President/Mr. Obama,
The best thing about living in the White House would be
running around like a maniac. The thing I would like least
is the work."

—HOLLY WONG, age 9, San Francisco[1]

Drive involves these items from chapter 12:

- ➡ **Focus:** Stays focused at meetings and at work on what's most important. Is fully present. Gives the right amount of detail to the right audiences.
- ➡ **Energy:** Projects physical, emotional, and mental energy (physical means you're animated; emotional, you care; mental, you're alert). Sustains energy over time.
- ➡ **Initiative:** Offers ideas and suggestions to continuously improve and innovate. Experiments with new approaches, takes calculated risks. Is proactive.
- ➡ **Commitment:** Makes and keeps commitments. Takes responsibility for getting things done. Stays true to one's values. Persists, persists, persists.

Focus: We've already devoted Part I of this book to focus. Here, we're also talking about being present. It's hard to have presence when you're multi-tasking or distracted.

Energy: Can you imagine a CEO without it? Where do you get your energy from? And how do you sustain it, day after day?

Energy and focus make a compelling pair. If you have energy without focus, you'll appear hyper-caffeinated and just get in everyone's way. But focus without energy is also a problem; you know what's important, but can't get moving.

Initiative and commitment also go together nicely. Initiative is about starting things, commitment is about finishing. Commitment is especially important—one of the fastest ways to build, or destroy, trust.

Presence Action #3: Focus

Stop Checking Email 74 Times/Day—Especially at Meetings

I didn't check email once, not for two weeks. I was on vacation at the time, but still.

How often do you check? For most of us, according to researcher Gloria Mark, University of California, it's 74 times/day.[2]

That means, during my two-week vacation, I didn't check email 1,036 times. I missed it.

One day, I noticed a newspaper article about email. "This article," I told my wife, "says that email will never die. Ever."[3]

"I thought you weren't supposed to be thinking about email," my wife said.

"I'm not checking it," I said. "I'm just reading about it. They call it 'the cockroach of the Internet'"[4]

"That's gross," my wife said.

Well, cockroach metaphors aren't for everyone. Some people don't like bugs of any sort.

Before vacation, I had a computer bug. A friend suggested a simple fix. "Reboot," she said. "When nothing else works, my solution is always the same: turn off the machine." Sure enough, that worked.

To stay focused at work, you need to turn off the machines periodically. Some of my clients ban phones during meetings. They add "tech breaks" in case people get desperate.

"I was surprised," a manager told me recently, "to discover how negatively people viewed my texting during meetings."

Maybe you can multi-task, maybe you can't (neuroscientists say you can't), but either way, it sends the wrong message.

It's not enough to pay attention. You've also got to look like you're paying attention (*optics*).

Presence Action #4: Energy

Before You Start Work, Warm Up

You present yourself every day, as discussed, even if you work at home.

And what you're presenting, always, is your mood, which others experience as positive energy, negative energy, or no energy.

"I can't have a bad day," says CEO Joseph J. Plumeri. "If I walk into a meeting, and I'm grumpy—not good . . . You simply can't have that one off day that's bad, because you're going to affect a lot of people."[5]

Energy is viral. We know that.

But, like the Dunkin Donuts commercial, we sometimes wake up wrong. It's too early and it's too dark. But too bad, time to make the donuts.

What's your morning mood? The typical morning involves:

- ➡ An alarm clock. I use one, and every time it goes off, I'm alarmed. I'm also alarmed by the possibility that it won't go off.
- ➡ Rush hour. You've probably engineered your morning with split-second precision. Extra time? None. Rush hour begins the second you step out of bed.
- ➡ World news. Let's face it, the news is not good. Typical headline: "Yesterday, something bad happened. Tomorrow, something even worse. Stay tuned."
- ➡ Your personal news. Everyone's got at least two or three concerns that they wake up into. What's bothering you, what's not working? Could be anything from your health, to your family, to your household appliances.

Meanwhile, you need to get to work (another concern: what to wear!). But first, let's warm up.

How? Lots of options: exercise, music, meditation. I do these things daily, even though that sometimes requires a 4:30 a.m. start. I especially like exercise; the more you sweat before work, the less you'll sweat during.

Looking for a faster warm-up?

1. Smile (time required: seconds).

Sure, you smile when you're happy, but research says it also works in reverse—smiling impacts your mood (*act as if*).

Details: Two researchers, Tara Kraft and Sarah Pressman, got some people in their experiment to smile, others not to, without anyone knowing whether he or she was smiling. (Long story, involved putting chopsticks in participants' mouths.)

Researchers then measured stress. Smiling, even for subjects unaware they were smiling, decreased stress.[6]

And if you like smiling, you could also . . .

2. Laugh (time required: seconds).

Sounds odd, I agree, and it's probably the last thing you feel like doing. Like smiling, the idea is to laugh for no reason, maybe in the shower or on your way to work. Laugh at your concerns and how, when you really think about them, they're no laughing matter.

Details: A physician in India, Dr. Madan Kataria, has been promoting the health benefits of laughing for many years. (Technically, you don't need to laugh for many years. A few seconds should suffice.)

There are 6,000 laughter clubs in 60 countries. I've never gone, nor is laughing-for-no-reason my usual practice. But occasionally, it's a useful warm-up. Especially when I'm in no mood.

3. Power pose (time required: two minutes).

Imagine two physical postures: an expansive posture (e.g., raise your arms toward the sky, V for victory), versus a contracted posture (e.g., lean over your smartphone). The first takes up space, the second doesn't.

According to research done by Amy Cuddy, a Harvard Business School professor, expansive postures, held for two minutes—before, not during an interaction—strengthen both your internal chemistry and your external impact.

Details: The expansive pose increases the dominance hormone (testosterone), while decreasing the stress hormone (cortisol). High dominance/low stress is a potent combo across the animal kingdom.

And Cuddy's research subjects who power posed outperformed their peers in mock interviews.[7]

The point is to bring your best self to work. If that's not the one you wake up into, warm up.

Move More, Sit Less

I like to pace. Sometimes I pace when I need to think about something difficult.

Pacing back and forth is a pleasant way to avoid thinking about something difficult—similar, I suppose, to saddling up a horse and galloping out of the office.

But I often get ideas this way.

Moving gives you mental, physical, and emotional energy. Want to change your mood? Try a fast 10-minute walk, suggests Robert Thayer, a psychology professor at California State University. Walking tops his list of mood boosters.[8]

To move more, invest in a really bad chair. Unfortunately, I've got a really good chair, with a cushy seat you could sit on forever. This chair is all wrong.

Your ideal chair is rock-hard and extremely painful. That's the kind you want, one you can't sit on.

p.s. I wrote all these ideas "in one sitting." I think it shows.

Identify Your "Evil Secret"

You can't sustain energy if your job doesn't fit, no matter how much pacing you do. What do you really want?

"The key to what you really want," says David Maister, a consultant and former Harvard Business School professor, "lies in something that you don't like to admit.

'I don't like to admit it but I need to be the center of attention.' Ok; find a job that will let you show off. 'I don't like to admit it but I really want to be rich.' Fine; go out and get rich.

"Play to your 'evil secrets,'" advises Maister, "don't suppress them."[9]

I'm sure there are exceptions, but most secrets aren't evil, they're energy.

The hard part: figuring out your secret. My early jobs seemed random, but they weren't. Take a look:

→ Mailman, New York City. Great job, several summers during college.
→ Encyclopedia salesperson, Boston. Terrible job right after college. I lasted 30 days.
→ Taxi cab driver, Cambridge. Ok job, but lots of negative feedback. When I drive, even now, passengers often become agitated. They seem desperate to escape.

Are you desperate to escape your job? Maybe you've suppressed your secret. Mine didn't become obvious until later, in business school.

Ed Schein, an MIT/Sloan School professor, had researched a concept he called "career anchors." Your career anchor, said Schein, is your number one priority at work.

Schein identified eight anchors. When I first saw the list, one anchor jumped out: autonomy.

(You can find the list by searching "Ed Schein's 8 career anchors.")[10]

Autonomy attracted me to those early jobs (outside the office, with minimal supervision), and then later to consulting. Autonomy was my "evil secret."

What's yours?

Notice what energizes you. Do more of that.

Presence Action #5: Initiative

Initiative: Take a Calculated Risk

"You don't follow the rules," my wife said, "for avoiding a shark attack."

We were eating lunch, reading the Sunday papers, and my wife had just read about a man who swam 400 yards off a Cape Cod beach, and then was almost eaten by a shark.[11]

Main rule: stay in shallow water.

Sharks have been on my list of concerns for years, at least since the movie *Jaws*. I've never actually seen a shark, but still, they're on the list.

Turns out, I can worry about anything.

Lyme disease is also on the list. And of course, snakes. Bees were never on the list, but they got there after a *Time* cover story about their disappearance. With bees, you can apparently worry about both their presence and their absence.

A lot of worry is about losing something you're fond of, such as your loved ones, or your health, or, in the case of sharks, your upper and lower body.

"Loss aversion," says Dan Ariely, author of *Predictably Irrational*, "means that our emotional reaction to a loss is about twice as intense as our joy at a comparable gain."[12]

So we'll go out of our way to avoid loss. That's why we'd rather hold on to a losing stock than bite the bullet and reinvest our money. And we'd rather hold on to a losing job than reinvest our energy.

But playing it safe can be dangerous, like sitting all day at the beach in the sweltering sun, never going near the water, but slowly dying of heat exhaustion because—let's face it—the sun can kill you.

When was the last time you took a calculated risk? Nothing reckless or impulsive. Not swimming 400 yards out, just getting your feet wet.

"They were waiting to be told what to do," said CEO Jim Donald, head of the hotel chain Extended Stay America. To embolden his 9,000 employees, he handed out "Get out of jail free" cards.[13]

His message: Take a chance. And if you screw up, that's ok.

What would you try if you knew you couldn't fail? Everyone's afraid. But some people act anyway.

p.s. "More Americans were killed by collapsing sinkholes (16) than sharks (11) between 1990 and 2006."[14]

Note to self: Update list. Add sinkholes.

Should You Consult Your Boss? Find Out

The other day a manager called for some advice. She wanted her employees to take more initiative and be more resourceful, but for some reason, they didn't get it.

Her problem reminded me of getting lost one day in Paris, while looking for the Seine River.

I asked a few people for directions. "Où est la Seine?" I said. No one had any idea. Apparently, they'd never heard of the Seine, or else they'd heard of it but just didn't want to discuss it.

I admit my French is terrible. "Pardon me," they may have thought I was saying, "I obviously can't speak a word of your language, so please, just shoot me. Then throw me in la Seine."

Eventually, I found the Seine on my own. It's 486 miles long, so it wasn't exactly hiding.

Do you ever feel lost at work?

You probably know people who can't tolerate being lost, even for a second. They ask their managers for help the minute they feel frustrated or unsure what to do next.

Other people probably should ask for help, but seem content to nibble a croissant, sip a café au lait, and wander around in circles.

Either extreme is dangerous. And some managers are extreme about giving direction: they either give too much or too little, regardless of employee or project.

When should you ask for direction, or get approval? If your manager hasn't been clear, take the initiative to find out.

Try this question (the earlier you ask, the better): "What sorts of problems do you expect to be consulted on, and which ones do you expect me to handle?"

Presence Action #6: Commitment

Only Make Promises You Can Keep—Then Keep Them

You and I make promises every day. "I'll call you by 5 p.m.," you say, or "I'll get you the info by Friday." But then we get sidetracked.

That's a broken promise.

I almost blew a major deal due to a broken promise.

My wife and I had sold our house—the close was later that morning—and the buyers, a young couple, just needed to do their final inspection.

We'd already moved out, so I shouldn't have even been there, but I had a few things to clean up and a few things to give the buyers, including an extra refrigerator.

The refrigerator worked fine, but even if it broke, it was still worth $50. That's what NSTAR, the electric company, pays you, then they haul it away for free. I don't know why they do that, but I also don't understand electricity. Does electricity require vast quantities of broken refrigerators?

When the buyers showed up, I wished them well, and was headed to my car—suddenly, the husband came running out.

"Hey," he said, "where's the bookcase?"

We'd sold the buyers some furniture, including a $20 bookcase. We'd also donated some furniture to charity. I suddenly realized a bad thing: the charity had, accidentally, taken the bookcase.

"I'm so sorry," I said and explained what had happened.

Then I made a mistake. "I wonder if we could just swap the bookcase for the refrigerator?" Seemed reasonable, $20 for $50.

"How do we even know the refrigerator works?" said the husband. You could feel the trust evaporating rapidly.

"Works fine." I also mentioned NSTAR and the $50.

The husband looked incredulous, like I was making the whole thing up. "It's obvious," his look implied, "that you know nothing about electricity."

"I really wanted that bookcase," he said.

So I wrote a check for $20, then left.

"I can't believe the husband did that," said our real estate agent when I told her later. I agreed.

But I was wrong. I had promised the bookcase, then broken my promise. A promise isn't rational (let's trade $20 for $50). A promise is emotional.

It's your word.

The fastest way to build trust is to make promises, then keep them. And the fastest way to destroy trust is to do the opposite.

When You Lose Your Balance, Get Back Up

I was leading a management workshop one day when suddenly a huge TV fell on my head.

It didn't just fall out of nowhere. The TV was on a tall stand, which I was moving to the side, when the whole thing tipped over. Not to brag, but usually you have to be about 5 years old to pull off this trick.

The TV knocked me to the floor. The workshop stopped for a few minutes while I dusted myself off. I felt embarrassed.

"Large objects," I remember thinking, "should never fall on your head in the middle of a workshop."

Oh well. It's easy to lose your balance, happens to everyone. The key question: how fast do you bounce back?

Top fashion model, Jessica Stam, tripped while walking down a Paris runway. "I fell and got back up" she said. "It happens, and it's no big deal."[15]

Franklin Roosevelt, paralyzed from the chest down, fell while being helped to the stage at the 1936 Democratic Convention. The papers of his speech went flying.

"Clean me up," he said to his aides, "and keep your feet off those damned sheets."[16]

Moments later, Roosevelt was at the podium, inspiring a live audience of 100,000. Most hadn't noticed his stumble.

Life knocks you down. We all know that. The call is to get back up.

CHAPTER 15

Temperament: Communicate that You've Got the Right Disposition

"The world breaks everyone and afterward many are strong at the broken places."

—ERNEST HEMINGWAY[1], novelist, journalist

Here are the temperament items from chapter 12:

➡ **Humility:** Admits and learns from mistakes. Seeks and values others' ideas and involvement. Listens with respect. Shares credit.

➡ **Command:** Takes the lead. Speaks up. Asserts oneself skillfully, without either aggression or undue concern for being liked or agreed with.

➡ **Optimism:** Takes a positive approach to problems and tasks. Imagines and communicates a positive, credible future state.

➡ **Composure:** Demonstrates calm under pressure. Handles stressful situations well. Thinks on one's feet, improvises. Uses humor appropriately.

Different organizations define temperament differently. Your organization, for instance, may strongly value humility—or not at all.

And we could add 100 other items to temperament (e.g., the My-ers-Briggs dimensions, the "Big 5" personality traits, or anything in-volving "emotional intelligence").

But let's keep it simple. What is it about your presence that makes others listen—or not listen? These four items suggest different possibilities.

Humility and command have a yin-yang relationship. The art is to avoid getting stuck in either.

When do you step back and involve others (humility), and when do you assert yourself (command)? People may tune you out be-cause you're too tentative (excess humility), or too bossy (excess command). So balance is important.

You communicate optimism by how you talk about the future. It's about hope. But the goal is not to be optimistic 24/7—overdo it, and you'll lose credibility. Plus, there are certain jobs and certain situa-tions where imagining the worst-case scenario is smart.

Composure is how you act under stress. That's a moment of truth, especially if others are stressed too—they'll remember your behavior.

Presence Action #7: Humility

Make Others Feel Important

"I've got to get to Boston tonight!" the airline passenger yelled at the gate agent.

American Airlines had just cancelled his evening flight out of Philadelphia. There was only one flight left, and he was trying to get on it.

"That flight is oversold," said the gate agent.

"What if I told you," said the passenger, still yelling, "that I'm a heart surgeon and have to be in Boston for a critical operation?"

The gate agent looked unimpressed.

"Suppose I told you," the passenger continued, now red in the face, "that I'm the president of American Airlines?"

Another passenger muttered: "I guess the medical career didn't work out."

I was standing nearby, intrigued by the heart surgeon/president of American Airlines and his motivational technique. He pretended that he was important and that the gate agent wasn't. Generally, that technique doesn't get you off the ground.

Consider the opposite approach.

The former CEO of JetBlue Airways, David Neeleman, used to help clean the planes once a week. He also helped unload luggage. And if he was on the flight, he served snacks and beverages.

All this makes an impression. Another airline CEO, the former head of (now defunct) People Express, used to say that when a passenger boards a plane and sees clutter, that single impression makes the passenger assume sloppy engine maintenance (*optics*).

What do you assume about David Neeleman? If he helped out once a year, you might assume it was a gimmick. But cleaning planes on a regular basis makes you assume something else, aside from "those planes must be extremely tidy—and have great engines!"

All jobs are important, his actions said, and so too are the people doing them.

"Let's just treat people nice," he told an interviewer. "Sometimes people don't deserve to be treated nice. But let's just do it anyway, because that's just the way we want to do business."[2]

p.s. Back to the heart surgeon/president of American Airlines. Somehow, he made it onto the plane that night. There were probably other important people on board as well. But due to bad weather, we never made it out of the airport.

The universe didn't seem to care.

Use the Law of Agreement

"That is without a doubt the stupidest idea I've ever heard," said the CEO of CBS, Leslie Moonves.

The idea was for a new show, *Survivor*. Moonves eventually aired the show and made a fortune. Later, he freely admitted his initial reaction.[3]

How do you react to others' ideas and concerns? Be careful, if you want to survive.

You may be tempted to mask what you really think. Big mistake. If everyone at a meeting does that, you get groupthink—a disaster when bad ideas aren't stopped (see page 145).

Then there's the opposite approach. "I have a bad reputation at my company for speaking my mind when I hear something dumb," an executive confided. "Any advice?" he asked.

I suggested the law of agreement, which comes from improvisational theater. If you're on stage and someone tosses out an idea, your first move is to welcome it.

I recently took an improv class, and the teacher told me to play a senile 90-year-old man. "You've got to be kidding," I thought. I see myself closer to a 30-year-old neuroscientist.

But, after the scene, the teacher said, "I have no trouble believing you have severe dementia."

(I told my wife about this later. She just nodded.)

The law of agreement, applied to work, means to first greet an idea, criticism, or question with something positive. You could say, "Here's what I like about that," or "here's what your idea makes me think about."

Then state your concerns.

Les Moonves could have said, "We're in a creative business, and your idea is certainly original. My concern is that no one will watch the show."

Greet an idea the way you'd greet a person. Some retail stores have professional greeters. Imagine a store with the opposite approach. They replace all the greeters with homicide detectives; instead of saying hello to customers, they frisk 'em.

HOMICIDE DETECTIVE TO CUSTOMER: Ever been here before?

CUSTOMER: No.

DETECTIVE: What about November 2, between 7–8 p.m.?

CUSTOMER: I don't think so.

DETECTIVE: Really? Up against the wall, buddy.

You can greet an idea with respect; that's different than endorsing it. And you can disagree without being disagreeable.

(More improv on page 153, *Composure*.)

Encourage "Spirited Debate"

"How could we have been so stupid?" asked President Kennedy.

When: April 1961, less than 100 days into his presidency.

What happened: Kennedy approved an invasion of Cuba. Over 1,400 Cuban exiles, equipped and trained by the CIA, landed at the Bay of Pigs. They were quickly defeated by overwhelming force.

"Most of us," Kennedy later said, "thought it would work."[4]

But that "most of us" was an illusion; in truth, participants were intimidated.

Secretary of State Dean Rusk didn't think it would work. The plan didn't have "a snowball's chance in hell of success," he later wrote. "But I never expressed my doubts explicitly."[5]

"Dumb." That's how Secretary of Defense Robert McNamara later described the plan. But at the time, he gave his approval.

Why didn't anyone speak up?

"One's impulse to blow the whistle on this nonsense," said Arthur Schlesinger Jr., Special Assistant to President Kennedy, "was simply undone by the circumstances of the discussion."[6]

Schlesinger sent Kennedy a private memo opposing the strike. But he stayed silent during group discussions.

"Groupthink," is how psychologist Irving Janis later described those discussions. No real debate or dissent. And no devil's advocate—a role that Robert Kennedy would later champion.

Instead, false agreement. Participants wrongly assumed that everyone else in the room agreed.

Ever been in a room like that?

After the failure, Kennedy sought advice from Dwight Eisenhower, his predecessor. And then, 18 months later, during the Cuban Missile Crisis (at least partly caused by the Bay of Pigs), Kennedy's team changed their approach.

What was Eisenhower's advice? You need spirited debate.[7]

Presence Action #8: Command

Leading a Meeting? Be the Conductor

The train conductor gave us a no-nonsense warning as we approached New Haven, CT. We were early, he said, so it was permissible to step off the train.

"But," he warned, "you've only got six minutes. We'll be leaving for NYC at 9:41 a.m. And that's 9:41 my time."

I admired the repetition of 9:41. And also the "THAT'S 9:41 MY TIME" part, which showed a take-charge attitude, spiked perhaps with just a dollop of insanity.

When was the last time you missed a train? Or a plane? Rarely happens, right? On the other hand, people are late for meetings all the time. More about that in a second.

Back to the train. I did get off because I'm one of those people who worry every time I read the latest research about excessive sitting.

("How did he die?" I imagine someone asking about me. "Oh, he took a train from Boston to NYC and never got up. Not once. And then, of course, he couldn't get up. For the main reason, he was dead.")

So I stepped off and did a few stretches, but I didn't go far because this was a train that could leave, really, at any second, based on the conductor deciding, purely on whim, "Off we go, it's 9:41—MY TIME!"

The next time you run a meeting, *be the conductor*.

What does that mean? Well, for one thing, be clear about when the meeting starts and when the break ends, and then—here's the tough part—stick to those times.

Sure, you may feel uncomfortable starting or resuming a meeting when people are missing. But that's what a conductor would do.

Be the conductor means to demonstrate command, to assert leadership. That doesn't mean you should dominate the discussion.

But when you're leading a meeting, sometimes you need to focus more on getting the train to the station, and less on getting all the passengers to love you.

p.s. If your meeting exceeds an hour (most meetings shouldn't), you definitely need a break—unless you want half the room to keel over from excessive sitting.

How to Lead a Meeting without Pulling Teeth

Sometimes I help managers run better meetings.

But in my private life, I've been trapped at several bad meetings—the kind where you squirm in your seat—with the dentist. Luckily, the dentist wasn't actually in the seat.

Is there a connection between good meetings and bad dentistry? Yes! It's about control.

Mistake #1: **Too much control. You talk, but no one's engaged.**

One day, I asked my dentist why he didn't have a spittoon. I like spittoons. They let you, the patient, sit up once in a while, spit, and take a break.

"I hate 'em," he said, almost to himself, "every single one of them." Was he talking about spittoons or patients?

I couldn't tell.

Before I could offer any more advice, he put a suction hose in my mouth. Clearly, this man had a schedule, and there was no time for spitting.

Fine. But you certainly don't want dead silence at your meetings. If you're doing all the talking, that's less like a meeting, more like a bad dental experience.

Why are you talking so much, anyway?

Probably because you've got too much info, too little time. Well, why not send some of that info in advance?

Avoid using your meeting to dump data. Instead, use the meeting to discuss and debate so that you (and/or the group) can decide and act.

Mistake #2: **Too little control. Everyone talks, but nothing gets done.**

I once had a dentist—or else it was someone pretending to be a dentist—ask me, "What are your goals for your teeth?"

I didn't really have any, other than to keep them. And I expected the dentist—or this person impersonating one—to provide a modicum of direction.

Same for the meeting leader. Without you steering, everyone may participate, but your meeting goes nowhere.

To maintain control, you don't need to dominate, but you do need to drive the structure. Begin with your purpose. What is it? And what decisions need to get made, and by whom? Be explicit.

Deputize a timekeeper—better if it's not you—to alert the group if the conversation goes off the rails.

And set some ground rules early to prevent trouble later. For example: no cell phones, no side conversations. And no spitting . . .

A good meeting is both efficient (uses time well) and engaging (uses people well).

To achieve both, flex control.

Push Back, without Being Pushy

I was trying to park at Logan Airport in Boston, Lot E. I love Lot E, for the main reason that it's outdoors, so you have at least a 50-50 shot of finding your car again.

Unfortunately, there was an attendant blocking the entrance. "Go to Lot E2," he said. "It's right next door."

That's true, but to get there you have to wind around the airport, which means, if you're me, you have an excellent chance of ending up in Rhode Island.

Ten minutes later, I wasn't in Rhode Island, but I also wasn't in Logan Airport. Somehow, I'd been shot out through the airport tunnel into South Boston. By the time I returned, Lot E2 was closed. The amusing part was that Lot E was now open.

My mistake. When the parking attendant said "no," I heard nonnegotiable.

When you get a "no" at work, or encounter an obstacle, how quickly do you fold?

In sales, you learn that "no" is often just an opening gambit. It never hurts to test or probe, as long as you're respectful. The parking attendant might have said yes, I'll never know.

The next morning, I was staying at a hotel with guest privileges to a nearby gym. I got a gym pass, then ran over. It was raining, so by the time I reached the gym, I was soaked.

I gave the receptionist my pass. "Unfortunately," she said, "we'll also need a photo ID."

But I'd learned my lesson from the day before. "Is there any way," I asked, "to just use the pass today? My driver's license is back at the hotel."

"No," she said. "You'll have to get the license."

I mentioned the weather.

Receptionist: "Sorry, you'll have to go back."

We were in the midst of "broken record," an assertiveness technique originally invented by children to get ice cream. It sounds like this:

CHILDREN: We want ice cream.

PARENTS: No.

CHILDREN: When can we have ice cream?

PARENTS: Not until the sun comes up.

CHILDREN: When will that be?

PARENTS: Never.

CHILDREN: Ice cream, ice cream, ice cream!!!

With broken record, you calmly repeat your position. Sometimes it works, other times you end up back in Rhode Island.

This time, the receptionist let me in. Our conversation had stayed friendly, but I decided not to ask for ice cream.

Your Job Isn't to Get Everyone to Like You— Do What's Right

The other day, I realized something alarming about myself.

I'd been thinking about U.S. presidents and their low approval numbers. "If I was interested in polling," President Obama once said, "I wouldn't have run for president."

Hmm. Is any U.S. president really immune to polls? George W. Bush, near the end of his presidency, was asked: "You're leaving as one of the most unpopular presidents ever. How does that feel?"

"I was also the most popular president," Bush said.[8]

That's true, Bush's approval numbers ranged from 25% to 90%, according to Gallup. Imagine a job where, Monday, everyone loves you; Tuesday, no one even likes you.

I definitely couldn't be president; that's obvious from a recent Saturday yoga class I attended.

"Is there anyone here," the teacher asked, "who's never done yoga?" She seemed to linger on the word *never*, as if the very idea was preposterous.

I was the only one. "Very unusual," she said to me. Then, during the class, she praised just about everyone: "Exactly right, Lisa," she'd say, or, "Lovely, Michael. You've really got it."

I was hoping she'd say, "Paul, I can't believe this is your first class, you're so natural!" But no, whenever she looked my way, she seemed to frown.

I pictured a besieged U.S. president, say, Abraham Lincoln, in my situation. Lincoln was reviled and ridiculed—he might have benefited from yoga. I imagined Lincoln standing on his yoga mat in the warrior pose, while his yoga teacher frowned. Would Lincoln have cared? Doubt it.

But I did.

"Care about what other people think," said the ancient philosopher Lao Tzu, "and you will always be their prisoner."

Maybe. But maybe part of you never stops caring. Maybe the trick, as in yoga, is simply not to get stuck in that position.

p.s. Of the last 11 presidents, Eisenhower through Obama (as of 2013), the American public now only rates three as "outstanding/ above average."

Kennedy gets high scores from 74%; Reagan, 61%; Clinton, 55%. Two of those men were shot; the other impeached.[9]

Presence Action #9: Optimism

Check Your Expectations and How You Communicate Them

If you ask my wife about my best traits, *flexible* won't be on her list. So I couldn't wait to tell her, one day, what a long-time client said.

"Apparently," I said, "I'm the most flexible consultant she's ever worked with."

"Apparently," my wife said, "she's never had lunch with you."

My wife has a point here. I'm the sort of person who orders salad "with dressing on the side," a tuna sandwich "without extra mayo," and iced tea "with very little ice."

But my client wasn't talking lunch. And she wasn't just complimenting me, she was subtly influencing me. "I value flexibility," she was basically saying. "Keep doing that."

How do you communicate expectations?

There's a big difference, for example, between saying to a child "if you go to college" versus saying, "when you go to college."

Suppose, as a manager, you believe in Theory X. That's what psychologist Douglas McGregor, years ago, called the expectation that employees are lazy and unmotivated.

Theory Y, according to McGregor, is the opposite expectation. And a Theory Y manager will create a different climate and get different results than a Theory X manager.

Sometimes you and I convey our expectations nonverbally, without even realizing it.

One disturbing study (take a breath here) involved rats. Lab technicians were given some rats, and then told they had to learn to run a maze.

To be clear, it was the rats who had to run the maze, not the lab techs. Although if I were a lab tech, I'd definitely learn to run the maze, or run the hallways, or run for my life—anything to escape the rats.

Some lab techs were told their rats were super-smart and would learn the maze quickly. Other techs were told the opposite. And, sure enough, the smart rats outperformed the stupid ones from day one.

But both groups of rats were the same. The only difference—in a Theory X, Theory Y way—were the lab techs' expectations.[10]

Your expectations influence behavior, yours and others, more than you think.

p.s. McGregor's point wasn't to be a Theory Y manager 24/7. Sometimes Theory X is justified.

p.p.s. For lunch, California Pizza Kitchen makes an excellent tortilla soup. But hold the extra tortilla chips.

Don't Screw Up

I was about to step on stage and give a keynote speech, when my client offered some last-minute advice:

"Don't screw up," he said.

As soon as I heard this, all I could think about was screwing up. "So what you're really saying," I replied, "is 'knock 'em dead.'"

"No," my client said. "What I'm really saying is, 'Don't screw up.'"

So I didn't. But I kept thinking about the tightrope artist, Karl Wallenda, who plummeted to his death from the high wire.

His wife later revealed that he had been unusually preoccupied with *not* falling.[11]

The mind has trouble with negatives. When someone tells you to not do something, it's hard to imagine the *not*, but easy to imagine the *something*.

Still, you can motivate others (or yourself) with either negative or positive outcomes.

The "don't screw up" negative method is powered by fear; you focus on avoiding the worst.

The "knock 'em dead" positive method is powered by hope; you focus on achieving the best.

Fear or hope—which do you prefer?

When my children were teenagers, I could hand them the car keys and either say, "Drive safely," or "Try not to smash the Toyota into a tree."

I usually advised them to drive safely. Then, later, I worried about the tree.

Presence Action #10: Composure

Getting attacked verbally? Use verbal judo.

Suppose your boss, or a key client, is unhappy with your performance. Your instinct is to debate and defend. Your instinct may be wrong.

The technique "yes and" comes from improvisational theater, which we just discussed. If you're an improv actor, your job is to agree.

"Be a tiger," the audience says.

You can't say, "No, I don't feel like a tiger today. I'm too bloated. I feel like an elephant, a big elephant in search of a low-fat, gluten-free diet."

"Yes and" starts with agreement.

Maybe you can agree with the facts. "You're right," you say. "I didn't meet expectations" or "That's not up to our standards either."

Maybe you can agree with the other person's feeling. "I know you're frustrated with me, and I'd like to understand why."

But if possible, agree on something.

At some point, you can also say, "I'm not sure I completely agree" (watch your tone of voice here). But listen first.

"Yes" can take many forms.

When asked a tough question: "I'm glad you asked that," or "Other clients have asked the same thing," or "I'd be wondering that too if I were you."

When attacked: "I appreciate your directness. Please go on."

All these things say "yes." What about simply saying, "I understand" or "Got it."

Unsatisfying. What, exactly, did you get? Suppose you get your spouse non-fat milk when she really asked for 2%. "Honey," you say, "I got it." But you didn't get the right thing, did you?

Saying, "Got it" is too fat-free. Go the extra 2%; confirm what you got.

When you offer your perspective—the *and* in "yes and"—you can either talk about the past (why this thing happened) or the future (what you're going to do about it). Or both.

When talking about the past: keep your explanation short. You might say, "We did underperform. Can I tell you what happened?"

Suppose there were 10 contributing factors. Just give the top two or three.

When talking about the future: say what you're going to do, but don't over-promise.

Avoid the word *but*. *But* is a killer, it negates everything. I agree with you *but* spells trouble. I agree with you *and* sounds better, even if you proceed to say the same thing.

You may be thinking, *Wait a minute, mister. There's no way this technique will work all the time.*

You're right! Techniques like this, done mechanically, sound hollow. You also need genuine intention—in this case, to find agreement. What can you agree on? Your critic isn't 100% delusional. Or is he?

p.s. One more thing: if the other person crosses the line from civility to abuse, change tactics.

Take Strategic Pauses

We already talked about pausing when giving a presentation (page 50, *Speed Up/Slow Down*). In addition, pause:

1. **When you get emotionally triggered.** Suppose your manager tells you about a promotion: "Sorry, you didn't get it. We chose Harriet."

    Harriet??? Count to 10. Still triggered? Count to 10,000. Pause before you say something unfortunate.

2. **After you ask a question.** Common mistake: rushing in with a dozen more questions before anyone has answered the first.

    "How come I didn't get the promotion?" you ask your boss. "Is it because of my leadership ability? My collaboration skills? Do you dislike my hair?"

3. **Before sending an email, especially an angry one:** "Re: Harriet's promotion: I'm repulsed and deeply nauseous."

    Pause. Is "deeply" the right word? Did you spell-check? Do you really need to "reply all"?

4. **Before answering a phone call.** Who's calling? Oh no, it's Harriet! Breathe. Smile. Then answer the call.

The Next Step

"Showmanship, George. When you hit that high note, say goodnight and walk off."

—JERRY SEINFELD,
(from NBC'S *Seinfeld*)

Practice

"When Barack Obama watched the video of the debate, he grimaced. 'It's worse than I thought' ran through his mind."[1]

It was 2008. Obama was just beginning his run for president. Although widely acknowledged as a gifted communicator, he knew he could do better.

That's how high-performers think, they commit to continuous improvement.

Four years later, after his first debate with Mitt Romney, President Obama probably grimaced again. Post-debate consensus: Obama lost badly.

Turns out, most U.S. presidents lose their first reelection debate.[2] One reason: lack of practice. Practice doesn't make perfect, it just makes you better. Anyone can have a bad night, what matters is what you do the next day.

What will you do next? Forget perfect, just pick one or two things to practice. Consider your next meeting, or your next conversation, or your next email. There are a lot of 8-second moments; you present yourself every day.

And whatever you practice, act as if your message matters. Because it does.

Then Let Go

Years ago, I did a series of TV commentaries for CNN's *Business Unusual*. Later, I hired an actress to critique my work.

The actress said some complimentary things, which I remembered for approximately 8 seconds. Then she offered some constructive advice:

"You need to be more like the actor Marlon Brando."

This I believed completely. I always believe corrective feedback, even when it makes no sense. Some might call that a character flaw, and, of course, I'd agree completely.

"Excuse me?" I asked.

"Marlon Brando was famous for mumbling. Sometimes he sounded like he had marbles in his mouth."

"You want me to put marbles in my mouth?" I asked.

"No," she said, "but you're over-enunciating the words. I want you to be more nonchalant. Brando's attitude was, 'Hey, I'm Marlon Brando! If you can understand what I'm saying, great; if not, too bad.'"

From this feedback, I derived a theory about peak performance. I call it "Loose-Tight."

Tight means setting high standards and striving to do your best. Tight is familiar to high-performers. Tight is your inner mountain-climber.

Loose means letting go and relaxing. Loose means, once the show starts, you go with whatever happens. Loose is your inner beach bum.

To be exceptional—whether you're in a high-stakes meeting or just doing your daily work—you need both.

Suppose you're giving a presentation. Tight means you'll be well prepared. But if you're too tight, you'll sound scripted and tense.

Loose means you'll be good at improvising. But if you're too loose, your audience will question your gravitas.

So you need the combination, but it's not a 50-50 split. Start with tight. Put in the time, effort, and practice to accelerate your performance.

Then, get some marbles.

NOTES

INTRODUCTION

1. "Microsoft Attention Spans," 2015.
2. "You Now Have a Shorter Attention Span Than a Goldfish," Kevin McSpadden, www.time.com, 5/14/15.

CHAPTER 1

1. Scott Spencer, *Men in Black*, Knopf, 1995.

CHAPTER 2

1. YouTube: "Oprah gives away cars."
2. www.winstonchurchill.org/resources/speeches/1941-1945-war-leader/103-never-give-in.
3. *In Defense of Food*, Penguin Press, 2008.

CHAPTER 3

1. Robert Bolton, *People Skills*, Touchstone, 1986.

CHAPTER 4

1. "Scotts CEO Reprimanded for Language," *The Wall Street Journal*, 6/3/13.
2. "Follow My Logic? A Connective Word Takes the Lead," 5/30/10.
3. "Goodbye Frustration: Pen Put Aside, Roth Talks," *New York Times*, 11/17/12.
4. Radicati Group, Email Statistics Report, 2015–2019.
5. InternetSlang.com.

CHAPTER 5

1. Adapted from *Naked at Work*, Paul Hellman, NAL Trade, 2002.

CHAPTER 6

1. Chip Heath, Dan Heath, *Made to Stick*, Random House, 2007.

CHAPTER 7

1. "Kurt Vonnegut on the Shapes of Stories," www.youtube.com.
2. Shell and Moussa, *The Art of Woo*, Penguin Books, 2007.
3. Richard Ford, *Canada*, Ecco, 2013.
4. Hellman, *Naked at Work*.
5. Hellman, "Into the Giga Jungle," *New York Times*, 12/26/98.
6. Hellman, "Summer Worries," *Boston Globe*, 8/11/89.
7. Hellman, "Me and My Delusions," appearing in *Mirth of a Nation: The Best Contemporary Humor*, Michael Rosen, Harper Paperbacks, 2000.

CHAPTER 8

1. *New York Times*, 6/9/07.
2. I first learned this distinction while working with the Forum Corporation, a premier leadership development company.

CHAPTER 9

1. *Harvard Business Review*, July–August, 2004.
2. *Time*, 10/6/14
3. Adam Bryant, "Corner Office," *New York Times*, 11/16/13.
4. "The Moment?" *Chicago Tribune*, 5/9/01.

CHAPTER 10

1. "Fed's Yellen Sets Course for Steady Bond-Buy Cuts," *Wall Street Journal*, 2/11/14.
2. Mark Hulbert, "Bear Markets May Not Be as Ferocious as They Appear," *Wall Street Journal*, 3/8/14.
3. "Obama and Congressional Leaders Discuss How to Move on Immigration," 11/8/14.
4. "From the White House, Beer We Can Believe In," *New York Times*, 10/16/12.
5. Theodore White, *The Making of the President 1960*, Harper Perennial Political Classics, 2009.
6. Alan Lakein, *How to Get Control of Your Time and Your Life*, Signet, 1989.
7. Douglas Adams, Pan Books, 1979.

CHAPTER 11

1. Lou Cannon, *President Reagan: The Role of a Lifetime*, Public Affairs, 2000.
2. Michael Palmer, *The First Patient*, St. Martin's Press, 2008.

CHAPTER 13

1. "Inside the Galleon Jury Room," *Wall Street Journal*, 5/14/11.
2. "Understanding 'Honest Signals' in Business," *MIT Sloan Management Review*, Fall 2008.
3. "Surgeons' Tone of Voice: A Clue to Malpractice History," *Surgery*, July, 2002.
4. Jim Kuhn, *Ronald Reagan in Private: A Memoir of My Years in the White House*, Sentinel 2004. (Jim Kuhn was the coat-advocating advisor.)

CHAPTER 14

1. Jory John, "Dear Sir Obama: Presidential Advice," *New York Times*, 1/16/09.
2. "A Company Without Email? Not So Fast," *Wall Street Journal*, 6/17/14.
3. "For Email Newsletters, a Death Greatly Exaggerated," *New York Times*, 6/29/14.
4. Quote from Jason Hirschhorn, CEO, ReDef.
5. Adam Bryant, "Corner Office," *New York Times*, 12/5/09.
6. "Grin and Bear It: The Influence of Manipulated Positive Facial Expression on the Stress Response," *Psychological Science*, 2012.
7. Amy Cuddy, TED talk: "Your Body Language Shapes Who You Are," www.ted.com.
8. *Calm Energy*, Oxford University Press, 2001.
9. davidmaister.com/articles/maisters-laws-of-the-job-search.
10. For additional info, including a self-assessment: *Career Anchors*, Pfeiffer, 2008.
11. "How I Survived a Shark Attack," *Boston Globe*, 8/18/13.
12. "Ask Ariely: On Sports, Giving, and Convenient Accounting," *Wall Street Journal*, 9/28/12.
13. "Memo to Staff: Take More Risks," *Wall Street Journal*, 3/20/13.
14. "Once Bitten, Twice Shy: Our Exaggerated Fear of Shark Attacks," *The Guardian*, 8/6/13.
15. "How to Walk Like a Model," *Wall Street Journal*, 3/20/08.
16. Jean Edward Smith, *FDR*, Random House, 2008.

CHAPTER 15

1. Ernest Hemingway, *A Farewell to Arms*, Scribner's, 1929.
2. "On the Record: David Neeleman," *San Francisco Chronicle*, 9/12/04.

3. Commencement Address, Boston University, 2006.
4. "The Lesson John Kennedy Learned from the Bay of Pigs," *Time*, 4/16/01.
5. Dean Rusk, *As I Saw It*, Penguin Publishing, 1990.
6. Arthur Schlesinger Jr., *A Thousand Days*, Houghton Mifflin, 1965.
7. Nancy Gibbs and Michael Duffy, *The Presidents Club*, Simon & Schuster, 2013.
8. Peter Baker, *Days of Fire*, Anchor, 2014.
9. Gallup.com, "Americans Rate JFK as Top Modern President," 11/15/13.
10. "Expectations May Alter Outcomes," *Wall Street Journal*, 11/7/03.
11. Warren Bennis, Burt Nanus, *Leaders*, Harper & Row, 1985

CONCLUSION

1. John Heilemann and Mark Halperin, *Game Change*, Harper Perennial, 2010.
2. Nate Silver's FiveThirtyEight, *New York Times*, 10/8/12.

INDEX

ABOUT PAUL HELLMAN

Paul helps business leaders make their point in an 8-second world.

He consults and speaks internationally, and has advised thousands of executives and professionals at organizations like Aetna, BIC, Biogen, Boeing, Bose, Kaiser Permanente, MFS Investment Management, NASA, New Balance, United Technologies, and many others.

Author of *Naked at Work: How to Stay Sane When Your Job Drives You Crazy*, and *Ready, Aim, You're Hired!*, he has written occasional columns for such newspapers as the *New York Times, Wall Street Journal, Washington Post*, and *Boston Globe*, as well as delivered public radio commentaries for *Marketplace*, and television commentaries for CNN's *Business Unusual. CNBC.com* has published dozens of his fast tips.

He holds a master's degree in management from MIT's Sloan School, and has led workshops for Sloan MBAs during the school's innovation week.

To contact Paul about speaking at your organization, or for more information about his training and consulting company, *Express Potential*®, please visit www.expresspotential.com or email info@expresspotential.com.